The Methuen Drama Book of Monologues for Young Actors

Edited with notes by

ANNE HARVEY

Preface by

JANE LAPOTAIRE

BLOOMSBURY

LONDON · NEW DELHI · NEW YORK · SYDNEY

Bloomsbury Methuen Drama
An imprint of Bloomsbury Publishing Plc

50 Bedford Square	1385 Broadway
London	New York
WC1B 3DP	NY 10018
UK	USA

www.bloomsbury.com

Bloomsbury is a registered trade mark of Bloomsbury Publishing Plc

First published as *The Methuen Audition Book for Young Actors* in
1993 by Methuen Drama
Reissued as *The Methuen Book of Monologues for Young Actors* in 2003
Title changed to *The Methuen Drama Book of Monologues for Young Actors* in 2007
Reprinted 2008, 2009, 2010, 2011, 2012, 2013, 2014

British Library Cataloguing-in-Publication Data
A catalogue record for this book is available from the British Library.

ISBN: PB: 978-0-4137-7279-4

Library of Congress Cataloging-in-Publication Data
A catalog record for this book is available from the Library of Congress.

Typeset by Hewer Text Composition Services, Edinburgh
Printed and bound in India

for

Marguerite (Rita) Beale

an incomparable drama teacher

and

Mary Greenslade

who knows all about drama anthologies

and

Michelle Frost

who helped make this one

Thank You

Contents

Preface by Jane Lapotaire   xi
Notes to the Actor   xv

AUDITION SPEECHES (arranged in order of age)   1

11–16

Male

Operation Elvis C P Taylor   3
Kes Barry Hines   6
P'Tang, Yang, Kipperbang Jack Rosenthal   8
Man in Motion Jan Mark   10
Carving a Statue Graham Greene   12
Clay Peter Whelan   14
The Moon's The Madonna Richard Cameron   16
Once a Catholic Mary O'Malley   18
My Children, My Africa Athol Fugard   20

Female

Random Thoughts in a May Garden James Saunders   22
Whistle Down the Wind Mary Hayley Bell   24
The Adoption Papers Jackie Kay   26
Invisible Friends Alan Ayckbourn   28
The Burston Drum Ellen Dryden   31
Tokens of Affection Maureen Lawrence   33
Bleak House Charles Dickens   35
Dreams of Anne Frank Bernard Kops   37
National Velvet Enid Bagnold   39
Daisy Pulls it Off Denise Deegan   41
All Things Nice Sharman Macdonald   43

The Two Noble Kinsmen John Fletcher and
   William Shakespeare   45
When We Are Married J B Priestley   47
Brand Henrik Ibsen   49
Brother in the Land Robert Swindells   51
A Boston Story Ronald Gow   53

17+

Male

Candida Bernard Shaw   57
Five Finger Exercise Peter Shaffer   59
Chains Elizabeth Baker   61
Hamp John Wilson   63
Not About Heroes Stephen Macdonald   65
Orphans Lyle Kessler   67
The Vortex Noël Coward   69
It's Ralph Hugh Whitemore   71
The Roses of Eyam Don Taylor   73

Female

The Gut Girls Sarah Daniels   75
Hindle Wakes Stanley Houghton   77
Same Old Moon Geraldine Aron   79
Vanity Fair William Makepeace Thackeray   81
The Black Prince Iris Murdoch   83
The Arcata Promise David Mercer   85
Shakers John Godber and Jane Thornton   87
Adam Bede George Eliot   89
Plenty David Hare   91
The Old Bachelor William Congreve   93
Keeping Tom Nice Lucy Gannon   95
A Woman Killed With Kindness Thomas Heywood   97
Hush April De Angelis   99
The Cagebirds David Campton   101

25+

Male

The Three Sisters Anton Chekhov   105
Love for Love William Congreve   107
Up'n'Under John Godber   109
Rope Patrick Hamilton   111
Son of Man Dennis Potter   113
Arden of Faversham Anon   115
Playing Sinatra Bernard Kops   117
Albert's Bridge Tom Stoppard   119
Breaking the Code Hugh Whitemore   121
The Gift of a Lamb Charles Causley   123

Female

Visiting Hour Richard Harris   126
The Rover Aphra Behn   128
Stage Door George S Kaufman and Edna Ferber   130
Summerfolk Maxim Gorky   132
The Winter Wife Claire Tomalin   134
Diana of Dobson's Cicely Hamilton   136
Bold Girls Rona Munro   138
Golden Girls Louise Page   140
Map of the Heart William Nicholson   142
My Mother Said I Never Should Charlotte Keatley   144
The Man Who Came to Dinner George S Kaufman and
    Moss Hart   146
Our Day Out Willy Russell   148
The Passing-Out Parade Anne Valery   150
Womberang Sue Townsend   153
Alas, Poor Fred James Saunders   155
Reserved David Campton   157
Ask for the Moon Shirley Gee   159

Play Sources   161
Acknowledgements   165
Useful Addresses   170

Preface

Nothing is more guaranteed to produce a groan or a recoil of dismay from would-be thespians in amateur dramatic societies, schoolchildren competing for a chance to shine and please Mum and Dad in the school play, or young actors struggling in an horrendously over-populated profession for that first job, than the word 'Audition'.

The pressure of performing alone on an empty stage, albeit for as short a time as two or three minutes, while 'they' out there in the dark of the auditorium assess and criticise, is monumentally daunting. Consequently the importance of the choice of speech for this Herculean task cannot be overstressed. The variety and range of pieces in this invaluable book, so excellently researched and chosen by Anne Harvey, go a long way to eliminate the difficulty of this chore.

All that is left for me to do perhaps is to offer a few practical hints from my experience, both as an actor and a teacher of drama.

Never forget the audition speech is your tool, your path to that coveted role, your acceptance into Drama School, the means to professional employment, and as such it must be chosen with much thought and great care.

Of course an audition is tougher than appearing in an entire play, where you are part of a developing story, with other actors to 'play ball' with, whose energy will feed yours and vice versa: where you all share responsibility for moving the play along and feeding its many rhythms and emotional demands; where the director has designated who moves when and where, and the set designer has shown you where all the furniture will be. But when you're auditioning, 'they' out there, in the blackness of the auditorium, are watching to see if you can be totally absorbed and concentrated and utterly unselfconscious about what you're doing alone up there on the stage; creating the world of the play around you with perhaps no more than a chair for company, and presenting the inner life and thoughts of the character you're portraying.

So how to make this lonely trial by jury easier? I would always recommend doing a piece from a play you've been in if possible. The moves, the windows, doors, exits and entrances, where the characters stood will be part of your being. But if you really are a beginner and haven't had experience? First and foremost choose a piece that you respond to instinctively. Something in you has to say 'yes' when you read it: 'yes, I know how that felt', 'yes, I understand this person'. Make no mistake about it, it is not possible to play someone you don't like. If they are 'wicked' you must understand why, and *like* them for it, but if you can't, beware. You might find yourself standing outside your character and commenting on it by portraying it at arm's length. If it doesn't travel through you, it's not worth much. Don't allow yourself to make value judgements on your character. Having taken all that on board, you then read the entire play. Not once. Not twice, but as many times as is possible. You have to know the play inside out to be able to play this minute bit of the whole frieze of the character at its fullest potential. You have to know why your character says what he/she does at that precise moment. What's the emotional/intellectual motor that provokes that speech.

Choose a piece that's right for your age. The profession is so overpopulated in these days of recession, that there are plenty of 50- and 60-year-olds to play their own age, however clever you are with the make-up. Stick to your own age group if you seriously want to work.

Apart from the advice already given, choose a piece that will show your vocal, emotional and physical range at its best. Don't forget the last especially. The audition speech is not an opportunity for verse speaking. Move! 'They' want to see how you live the physical life of the character as well. So many young actors fall foul of this point and stand rooted to the stage, as if they had lost the use of their legs. Be brave. Be bold. Show yourself at your best. The theatre is a place for daring and courage.

A large selection of the pieces in this book are from relatively unknown plays, no small advantage to the young actor, encouraging a free rein to the imagination, knowing there is no yardstick of previous well-known interpretations against which they can be measured.

For the male actor, the range of parts offered varies from the sadly topical, poignant speech of Michael's, accused of child abuse, in *The Moon's The Madonna*, the naturalistic idiom of *Kes*, and the demanding verse of Causley's adaptation of the Wakefield Shepherds' play.

There is also ample opportunity for a variety of accents: South African for Athol Fugard's *My Children My Africa*; American for Eugene in *Brighton Beach Memoirs* and German for Walter in *Five Finger Exercise*. There's a style of bearing and 'period' deportment necessary for Jeremy in *Love for Love*, for Marchbanks in *Candida* and for the elegant, clipped 1920's passion of Rupert in *Rope* and Nicky in Noël Coward's *The Vortex*.

For the female actor the choice is even greater, for once here is a book with a preponderance of female roles, a rare beast indeed! There's the warmth and North Country wit of Ruby Birtle, the heightened verse of Gerd in *Brand*, the untypical 'feminism' of the independent straight-talking Fanny in *Hindle Wakes* to the common brashness of Irish Bella in *The Same Old Moon*. There's a chance for period style with Becky from *Vanity Fair*, Anne in *A Woman Killed With Kindness* and the Gaoler's Daughter from *Two Noble Kinsmen*.

Anne Harvey has researched her book exhaustively from novels as well as plays. The scope is enormous. The choice is yours. Choose wisely and well. Show yourself to your best advantage. Feel comfortable. Have fun, and Good Luck!

Jane Lapotaire
London, September, 1992

Notes to the Actor

Jane Lapotaire has given you some excellent advice in her introduction, and I only want to add a little to that.

Firstly, although I know the advantages of a collection like this to an over-worked teacher or busy student, I hope it won't prevent you looking further afield for audition scenes. Most of the plays I have selected contain other suitable extracts for both sexes: I hope too that they will inspire you to look for other plays by the same writers, or of a similar period. As with all the books I have edited over many years, this one could have been three or four times the length: in the end one has to be ruthless and make a final choice. But in libraries and book-shops (second-hand ones especially), and on other people's bookshelves are plays waiting to be used and adjudicators, directors and examiners will warm to an unusual and unexpected choice. Novels, too, often yield a good dramatic speech, and you will see that I have drawn from some of those for this book.

Although Jane Lapotaire has stressed the importance of reading the entire play I will stress it again. As an examiner and adjudicator, nothing makes me more furious than the unprepared student with the feeble excuse: 'My teacher didn't tell me I had to read the whole play.' (Liar!) 'My friend had the only copy and forgot to give it to me.' (Or did you forget to ask?) 'I've got so much homework I haven't had time to read the play.' (Really?) 'Well, I haven't actually read it, but someone told me the story, so . . .' (So what?!) I won't go on, although I could! Those excuses are not fictitious. I have seen young (and older) actors mistake the period, the style, the setting, the character's age, size, and intention, movement, use of language and more, all because they had not bothered to read the whole play. Quite apart from letting yourself down, it is an insult to the playwright. Also, it is so rewarding to understand your chosen character in depth; what can be learnt through literature adds to an actor's personal development, to an understanding of people and life.

The plays and novels used in the anthology are available at the time of going to press, but it often happens that titles go out of print suddenly. At the back of the book you will find a list of addresses that could be helpful in searching for plays.

The support I have had from the editorial staff of Methuen has been unfailing, and my warm and grateful thanks go to Pamela Edwardes, Peggy Butcher and William Powell. Playwrights, their agents and publishers have shown interest in my work and here I must mention the constant help, advice and friendship I have always received from the staff of Samuel French Ltd, most notably Amanda Smith and Martin Phillips who shared their knowledge and expertise from start to finish.

Anne Harvey

11–16

Male and Female

Operation Elvis
C P Taylor

Malcolm, a schoolboy, lives in a fantasy world where he thinks he is Elvis Presley, the singer. This does not please his mother, her boyfriend, or the Headmaster. A crazy idea of leaving home for Elvis Presley's birthplace, Memphis Tennessee, results in Malcolm meeting Michael, a severely handicapped boy in a wheelchair. This new relationship helps him to an awareness of his own worth.

This speech comes just after the nurse in charge of Michael has told Malcolm that he must not consider taking the boy out in a boat (although later in the play this is made possible).

Setting: Outside the hospital, in Morpeth, near Newcastle-upon-Tyne.

Time: The present.

MALCOLM (*to* MICHAEL). Michael, I got a book on how to play the guitar so I could learn to play some of the tunes you like. (MICHAEL *ignores him.*) It's called *A Tune a Day*. It's good, I'm going to learn to read music and everything. Alex says he's going to pay for lessons for us. (MICHAEL *still ignores him.*) Will I wheel you round for a bit? (*Nothing.* MICHAEL *ignores him.*) Look man, she's right. Don't want to get you rotten drowned. (*No response.*) You going to speak to us? Look if you don't speak to us I might as well go home. I came out tonight especially to tell you, Michael, man *I couldn't help it* I mean, she's a Sister and everything.

MICHAEL *deliberately with all his strength spits in MALC's face.*

Filthy rotten pig! (*Wiping the spittle from face.* MICHAEL *is babbling in real anger.*) Rotten come here all the way to see you. (*Gripping him.*) Could rotten chin you, deserve it, rotten filthy dirty pig. (*Shaking him.*) (*To* AUD.) Could've rotten murdered him. That temper I've got. In the end I kind of stopped myself. I let go of him and started to go off without speaking to him. Rotten hating him. (*Shouting.*) Rotten stupid filthy cripple. I just turned away, going off. Sock! Then I remembered I'd left the stupid brake off his stupid chair and I didn't want it to start rolling down the hill, or anything. I went back to him, and he was just sitting there, not making any noise . . . but down his cheeks, two tears were going down. From his eyes. I'd never had that feeling before . . . looking at him, and there were two tears running down his face. (*To* MICHAEL.) What's the matter, Michael? I didn't hurt you man. What you crying for man? (*To* AUD.) I wiped the tears off his face with my hand and two more rotten tears came. (*To* MICHAEL.) Stop it man, what you crying for? Stop rotten crying! Look man, I'm sorry, its just my temper. Me Mam says when I lose me temper, I could kill somebody. I'm sorry. Look, she just got us all mixed up. You're still my friend aren't you man? Come on, I'm still yer friend amn't I? Look I want to go in the boat with you as much as you do, man. (MICHAEL *is calm now.*) Look, listen first day it's hot, right are you listening? Well Jackie and me'll organise it. Right? Jackie's got a friend with a van. We'll go out on that lake, right? It'll be safe, I mean, you should see what Jackie's made. Lifts us right up in the air. First time we tried it, mind, landed us right on me bum. Still black and blue from that.

MICHAEL *is smiling now. He is moving his arms, trying to control them, looking down at them* MALC *takes his hand.*

Right, we friends, now? (MICHAEL *is smiling.*) Mind, you're as bad as me, aren't you. Rotten temper you've got. (MICHAEL *is laughing with his eyes now.*)

4

Well you can burn my house, steal my car,
drink my liquor from my old fruit jar,
Do anything you want to do, but, ugh huh honey,
Lay off my shoes.
Don't you step on my blue suede shoes,
You can do anything but lay off my blue suede shoes.

Kes
Barry Hines

Written in 1968 and set in Barnsley, Yorkshire, this is the story of 14-year-old Billy Casper, and his kestrel hawk. The character of Anderson, another 14-year-old schoolboy, is a minor one; he appears during a scene in Billy's school when the teacher asks the boys to describe some 'real happening' in their lives. 'Anything at all, Anderson . . . Everybody remembers something about when they were little. It doesn't have to be fantastic, just something that you've remembered . . .'

ANDERSON. Well it was once when I was a kid. I was at Junior School, I think, or somewhere like that, and went down to Fowlers Pond, me and this other kid. Reggie Clay they called him, he didn't come to this school; he flitted and went away somewhere. Anyway it was Spring, tadpole time, and it's swarming with tadpoles down there in Spring. Edges of t'pond are all black with 'em, and me and this other kid started to catch 'em. It was easy, all you did, you just put your hands together and scooped a handful of water up and you'd got a handful of tadpoles. Anyway we were mucking about with 'em, picking 'em up and chucking 'em back and things, and we were on about taking some home, but we'd no jam jars. So this kid, Reggie says, 'Take thi wellingtons off and put some in there, they'll be all right 'til tha gets home.' So I took 'em off and we put some water in 'em and then we started to put taddies in 'em. We kept ladling 'em in and I says to this kid, 'Let's have a competition, thee have one welli' and I'll have t'other, and we'll see who can get most in!' So he started to fill one welli' and I started to fill t'other. We must have been at it hours, and they got

6

thicker and thicker until at t'end there was no water left in 'em, they were just jam packed wi'taddies.

You ought to have seen 'em, all black and shiny, right up to t'top. When we'd finished we kept dipping us fingers into 'em and whipping 'em up at each other, all shouting and excited like. Then this kid says to me, 'I bet tha daren't put one on.' And I says, 'I bet tha daren't.' So we said we'd put one on each. We wouldn't though, we kept reckoning to, then running away, so we tossed up and him who lost had to do it first. And I lost, oh, and you'd to take your socks off an' all. So I took my socks off, and I kept looking at this welli' full of taddies, and this kid kept saying, 'Go on then, tha frightened, tha frightened.' I was an' all. Anyway I shut my eyes and started to put my foot in. Oooo. It was just like putting your foot into live jelly. They were frozen. And when my foot went down, they all came over t'top of my wellington, and when I got my foot to t'bottom, I could feel 'em all squashing about between my toes.

Anyway, I'd done it, and I says to this kid, 'Thee put thine on now.' But he wouldn't, he was dead scared, so I put it on instead. I'd got used to it then, it was all right after a bit; it sent your legs all excited and tingling like. When I'd got 'em both on I started to walk up to this kid, waving my arms and making spook noises; and as I walked they all came squelching over t'tops again and ran down t'sides. This kid looked frightened to death, he kept looking down at my wellies so I tried to run at him and they all spurted up my legs. You ought to have seen him. He just screamed out and ran home roaring.

It was a funny feeling though when he'd gone; all quiet, with nobody there, and up to t'knees in tadpoles.

P'Tang Yang Kipperbang
Jack Rosenthal

Alan Duckworth is 14 and a pupil at a co-educational school. He has all the usual adolescent worries about growing-up, and at present his life is a mixture of cricket and appearing in the school play, opposite the girl he loves, the unattainable and lovely Ann. In this scene, which takes place outside Ann's house, she has been friendlier than before, and this gives Alan courage.
Time: The late 1940's, after the Second World War.

ALAN (*looking at* ANN. *He speaks quietly, solemnly, completely unselfconsciously, and very, very simply*). You're beautiful, Ann. Sometimes I look at you and you're so beautiful I want to cry. And sometimes you look so beautiful I want to laugh and jump up and down, and run through the streets with no clothes on shouting 'P'tang, yang, kipperbang' in people's letterboxes. (*Pause.*) But mostly you're so beautiful – even if it doesn't make ME cry it makes my chest cry. Your lips are the most beautiful. Second is your nape . . . (*After she queries this word.*) The back of your neck. It's termed the nape. . . . And your skin. When I walk past your desk, I breathe in on purpose to smell your skin. It's the most beautiful smell there is . . . . It makes me feel dizzy. Giddy. You smell brand-new. You look brand-new. All of you. The little soft hairs on your arms. . . . But mostly it's your lips. I love your lips. That's why I've ALWAYS wanted to kiss you. Ever since 3B. Just kiss. Not the other things. I don't want to do the other things to you. (*Pause.*) Well. I DO. ALL the other things. Sometimes I want to do them so much I feel I'm – do you have violin lessons? . . . (ANN *is rather thrown by this.*) . . . On the violin. (*She doesn't.*)

8

Well, on a violin there's the E string. That's the highest pitched and it's strung very tight and taut, and makes a kind of high, sweet scream. Well, sometimes I want you so much, that's what I'm like. . . . (*A pause*. ANN *thanks him for this remark*.) . . . I always wanted to tell you you were lovely. Personally, I always think it's dead weedy when Victor Mature – or whatsisname – Stewart Grainger – or someone says a girl's lovely. But you are. (*Pause*.) And I know girls think it's weedy when boys call them sweet. But you are. (*Pause*.) I don't suppose I'll ever kiss you now in my whole life. Or take you to the pictures. Or marry you and do the OTHER things to you. But I'll never forget you. And how you made me feel. Even when I'm 51 or something.

Man in Motion
Jan Mark

*Fourteen-year-old Lloyd has moved with his mother and sister
to the city, which means a new school and new friends and
a chance to develop his greatest enthusiasm, American football.
When Lloyd finds his loyalties are being tested he confides in the
family's new lodger, art lecturer, Paul Tyson. This speech is taken
from the novel.*
   Time: The present.

LLOYD. . . . Yes. I have got something on my mind. . . .
There's this boy I know, Keith Mainwaring; I met him
down at American football, and we got friendly. I mean,
we were friends right off, and his dad gives me a lift home
afterwards. He's really friendly . . . but he says things,
they both do . . . . Racist things. All the time, like without
thinking. Every time they see somebody Asian, they say
something . . . and I don't say anything. I don't know what
to say. I keep thinking they don't really mean it, especially
Keith, because he's nice, really, I mean, otherwise he's nice.
He rings up and asks how I am, and paid for my lunch and
that. I really like him, except for what he says. . . . That's
why I've stopped going to practices; to avoid him. I don't
think he really means it, I think it's just because of what
his dad says. Like my friend Vlad – from school, like he
said; if you're sexist it's because you've been brought up
to think like that, you never get the chance to work it
out. And I don't think Keith knows any Asians. He lives
up at the Highbridge end. . . . It's funny . . . ODD . . .
calling somebody a racist. It doesn't sound real. We have
this lesson at school, Social Awareness Studies, only we

call it Isms. Because that's what it is, all the time; sexism, racism, feminism. And last week we had this discussion on racism, somebody brought in a cutting from a newspaper, and everyone said how awful it was, only we've got these two girls in our class, Farida and Farzana, and nobody thought about them. They just sat there, and nobody took any notice or asked them what they thought, I mean, they never say much anyway, but that wasn't the point. Racism's just something half of us argue about while the other half do our homework. It's just a word. It doesn't mean anything, because it doesn't happen to us. . . . I think most of us are against it . . . . It's the first time I've had to do anything about it. Where we lived before, everyone was white anyway. If I'd met Keith there I'd never have known what he thought because he'd never have said anything. Racism was just something on the news. . . . But it's not for me. Not any more.

Carving A Statue
Graham Greene

Graham Greene describes his play as 'not realistic'. It is set in the South London studio of a not very good sculptor, a man obsessed by great Biblical subjects, out of fashion. The place is fairly bare, containing a tall ladder, a rough stone block surrounded by scaffolding, a statue, work bench, magic lantern and improvised screen. The boy, aged about 15 or 16, has been showing some of his father's slides on the screen, whilst talking to him.
   Time: 1960's

BOY. Last night I saw a child crying in a room across the street. He must have had a nightmare. Sometimes I have one too. Do you ever have a nightmare, father? . . . I used to be scared when I was alone in the house. . . . Sometimes I woke crying like that child. Years ago, when I was young, of course. . . . The door opened and a man came out. He picked the child out of bed and set him on his knee. I think he was telling a story because presently I could see them laughing. It must have been a terribly good story. Do you suppose he was the father? . . . Here's a box marked V, father. Was that when you were planning to carve a virgin? . . . Where are you going, father? Can I come with you? . . . Is mother's picture in the box marked V? . . . Which is mother's picture? . . . Please, father, which slide? . . . Good night, father. I expect I'll be asleep when you get back.

The father is gone. The BOY *hesitates a moment and then opens the box. He takes out the slides: there are only three of them. He tries holding one of them up to the light, but the light is not sufficient. He turns on the lamp of the lantern again and turns out the light of the studio and inserts a slide. What*

appears is some banal reproduction from a Murillo painting –
a lifeless sentimental face of a Virgin and Child. He gives a
sigh, a shake of the head, and substitutes a second slide. This
is a photograph of a little dead girl spread-eagled in a road –
perhaps it is a blitz photograph, perhaps one from the Spanish
War, perhaps from the battle of Warsaw. The BOY *exclaims*
with horror and approaches the screen. He stares a long time at
the picture, then kneels before it and tenderly touches the face.

Who are you? Are you alive? No, you're dead, aren't you?
Dead as mutton. Dead as a door-nail. Dead as mother. Or
are you asleep? Be asleep and I'll tell you a story, and when
you wake up, you'll be happy again. I'll tell you about my
father. He's big and strong and gentle too. For nine hours
every day he lives up there, thinking of God and every
evening he comes down here to me and we talk to each
other. About everything in the world. Have you a father?
He can be your father too. He's a man as high as a mountain
– (*He looks up towards the head of the statue out of sight.*) – with
a heart as deep as a lake. Nothing bad ever comes where he
is, and nothing will ever hurt you again. You'll be safe here.
There are no sudden noises to frighten you, and the rushing
cars are faint and far away on the road to Reigate. He'll say,
'Stay with us forever', and you'll say 'Forever' and the man
as high as a mountain. . . . Oh, sakes, sweetheart! I could
do with a woman in the house! (*His face close to child on*
screen.)

Clay
Peter Whelan

Sixteen-year-old Jimmy lives with his parents and elderly grand-mother in a converted hill farm turned pottery studio on the Staffordshire Derbyshire borders. Close friends of his parents' youth come to stay, upsetting the settled existence and here one of them, Win, tries to make Jimmy talk about the figures he moulds from clay.
   Time: The present.

JIMMY. I haven't got any. I got rid of them. There's no point in it is there? Not now. Who's going to see it? There won't be anyone left to see it. They'll be wiped out. Everyone'll be dead. How can anyone see it? There won't be any eyes. People are in a dream about it. They think there's going to be life – there won't be any life. There won't even be any worms. They'll be cooked in the ground. That's what makes it difficult . . . making the figures. I mean . . . you know what to do if someone's going to see them. But if no one is . . . how d'you go about it? There's no precedent for that. I don't destroy them. I don't break them up . . . I bury them. On the moor. I read about that Chinese Emperor whose tomb they've been digging up. They've found all these clay soldiers, full height, a whole army of them that he'd had buried to protect his tomb. They've dug out, I don't know how many, nine hundred of them and they're still finding more. I didn't want to make soldiers. I mean they're not to protect anything. Just people. Ordinary. Sitting up or leaning on one hand . . . looking. I tried to think where else there was where someone had made something not to be seen. I knew
14

Navajo Indians make patterns in sand for their ceremonies and then destroy them after it's over, but that isn't the same. That's like saying: the spirits see them, which is like saying: God sees them. But if you believed in God . . . if you believed in the Bible, then you'd know it had all got to end . . . like in the Book of Revelations. It ends. There's a day when it ends. Isn't there? . . . So I thought . . . go back before Christ, and there's those people's shapes they found at Pompeii. Those who were dying in the ash from the volcano. That got covered in a hard crust of ash . . . so you could pour in plaster and fill the shape they'd left behind, the moment they suffocated and died. Now, if you thought of them as figures . . . statues . . . not people . . . then they were not made to be seen! So what I do is I shape figures like them . . . so that they're looking into the blinding flash just before they die. Then I give them a first firing. What you call 'biscuit'. And then, I bury them out there so the sudden heat from the blast will be the second firing. Well no one's known temperatures let loose like that. The stones round them could vitrify and turn into glass. Then even if the clay shatters into dust the shape will still be there. In glass! (*He falters. Stops.*) I've only made twenty-three. Twenty-three! You'd have to make millions. The whole human race!

The Moon's The Madonna
Richard Cameron

The play describes the devastating effects of the wrongful accusation of sexual abuse on two children in a family. Michael, 16, half-brother to Danny and Shari, is under suspicion. A gentle, uncomplicated, unsophisticated boy, he works in Asda, the local supermarket. In this scene, set in the family home, he is talking to his older brother, Tom.
Time: The present.

MICHAEL. Will I have to make a statement? . . . What if I start getting mixed up? They might think I'm lying. If they think I'm frightened they might think I'm guilty . . . . Will they have a tape recorder? . . . I've seen them tape recorders. And if you don't say what they want you to say, you have to stay there until you do. I've seen it! . . . Will they tell Asda? I hope they don't. I don't want to lose my job now I'm working inside. I get on with everyone really well. . . . Can they find out? . . . They've got it all down on paper. They've got it on files. They keep them for years. . . . I haven't done nothing but I can't make them believe me. I wouldn't do anything to hurt Danny and Shari. I love them both. They kept saying about them not being my proper brother and sister, only half, about different dads, and how having a different dad might mean I thought of them different. That's all wrong, though, because we all belong to Mum, don't we? I couldn't hurt them. They kept saying about me not having a girlfriend. Why had I got no friends? Why did I stay in all the time? I don't want friends. I just want to look after Mum. I love her. And I want to help her. I had to tell them about her not

16

having a nice life with Danny and Shari's dad. About him making her frightened sometimes and not letting her go out anywhere. I said how I stayed in now, to help her. She's my Mum and I love her. . . . They said that maybe I stayed in so I could be with Shari. So I could have a cuddle. . . . I don't think they like families to have a cuddle.

Once A Catholic
Mary O'Malley

*While Mary McGinty, one of the more sophisticated members of
The Convent of Our Lady of Fatima's 5th Form, is on a school trip,
her boyfriend, Derek, gets involved with the less attractive, rather
innocent Mary Mooney. In this scene, Derek, a tall thin Teddy boy
in his late teens, is pacing up and down, smoking, trying to explain
himself to Mary McGinty. The scene takes place in Derek's house,
somewhere in the Willesden area of London, in 1977.*

DEREK. Look I've told you a hundred times, she didn't
mean nothing. And I didn't do nothing neither. Nothing
much anyway. I mean, be fair. She come up and spoke
to me in the street. I never knew her from Old Mother
Hubbard, did I? You know how it is when I get me attacks
of neuralgia. My eyesight gets affected, don't it. I couldn't
make out what she looked like in the street. She could have
been a really beautiful bird for all I knew. When I got her
inside the house and see what she really looked like I had
to draw the curtains double quick. I should have known
that was asking for trouble, though, 'cos once you're in
the dark with somebody it might just as well be anybody,
you know how it is. Oh, no, you don't, of course. Well I'm
only human, know what I mean? Not like you. No. You're
about as warm as a Lyons choc ice you are, darling. It's
about bleedin' time you faced up to the fact that I've been
impairing me capabilities for the sake of respecting you.
It's a wonder I ain't done myself some sort of permanent
mischief. Not that I get any credit for it, oh no. It's all
been a bleedin' waste of time. It's quite obvious you don't
wanna go out with me no more. You don't have to say it.
18

I'm going by the way you're acting towards me. I mean, I don't go looking for it, darling. But if it happens to come my way . . . I can't very well help myself, can I? And who in this world would blame me the way you behave towards me. You know my old Nan was half Italian, don't you?

My Children, My Africa
Athol Fugard

Thami, a black South African boy and Isabel a white South African girl meet as opponents in an inter-school debate. Mr M, principal of Thami's school, Zolile High, is inspired to coach them as a team for a big English Literature quiz. Their intelligence and eloquence has impressed him. A caring relationship develops between the three, but when Thami becomes involved in a political movement set up by his comrades from the location he is forced to break off his friendship with Isabel because she is white. When the mob riots through the streets demanding freedom they find Mr M, who has been accused of informing to the Government, and murder him. Thami, who was involved in the riot, comes to explain to Isabel the reasoning behind the killing and to say goodbye to her.

THAMI (*abandoning all attempts at patience. He speaks with the full authority of anger inside him*). Stop, Isabel! You must keep quiet now and listen to me. You're always saying you want to understand us and what it means to be black . . . well if you do, listen to me carefully now. I don't call it murder, and I don't call the people who did it a mad mob, and, yes, I do expect you to see it as an act of self-defence – listen to me! – blind and stupid but still self-defence. He betrayed us and our fight for freedom. Five men are in detention because of Mr M's visit to the police station. There have been other arrests and there will be more. Why do you think I'm running away? How were those people to know he wasn't a paid informer who had been doing it for a long time and would do it again? They were defending themselves against what they thought was

20

a terrible danger to themselves. What Anela Myalatya did to them and their cause is what your laws define as treason when it is done to you and threatens the safety and security of your comfortable white world. Anybody accused of it is put on trial in your courts and if found guilty they get hanged. Many of my people have been found guilty and have been hanged. Those hangings *we* call murder!

Try to understand, Isabel. Try to imagine what it is like to be a black person, choking inside with rage and frustration, bitterness, and then to discover that one of your own kind is a traitor, has betrayed you to those responsible for the suffering and misery of your family, of your people. What would you do? Remember there is no magistrate or court you can drag him to and demand that he be tried for that crime. There is no justice for black people in this country other than what we make for ourselves. When you judge us for what happened in front of the school four days ago just remember that you carry a share of the responsibility for it. It is your laws that have made simple, decent black people so desperate that they turn into 'mad mobs'.

ISABEL *has been listening and watching intently. It looks as if she is going to say something but she stops herself.*

Say it, Isabel. (*She refuses*). This is your last chance. You once challenged me to be honest with you. I'm challenging you now.

Random Thoughts in a May Garden
James Saunders

David and Sophie, a middle-aged couple with grown-up children, have recently bought an old house with a rambling garden. While moving in they come across an old, torn family photograph, the remains of which shows two little girls. While the couple are entertaining friends, philosophising on the meaning of life and the inevitable passage of time, we hear the voices of the little girls, Katie and Anne, speaking from the past. Katie is only about 11, the younger of the two, but an observant, mature-thinking child. She is sitting quite still.

Time: The present, although the photograph is set in Victorian times.

KATIE. I think there's a fly on the back of my hand. Walking. I can't look down. I can't even flap my hand or swat it or I shall come out blurred and I'll get the blame for spoiling the photograph. 'Anne sat still, see how still Anne sat, why couldn't you sit still like everyone else?' Well, I can. I don't want to be called Katie fidget whenever they show it to anyone. I can just imagine, how awful. I'd go through the whole of my life with it. The perfect photograph in memory of the wedding of *dear* Emily – where is she now, why isn't she in the photograph, it's her wedding? – only there in the corner *little* Katie all blurred. 'What a fidget, Katie fidget, she always was a fidgety child.' I wonder if Georgie will fidget. They've sat Georgie on the other side. He was standing behind me, he put his bony chin on my shoulder-blade and moved it about, it hurt, I told him to get off. I'd have shrugged my shoulder up only I was afraid he'd bite his tongue. That was considerate of me, only I'm afraid nobody will know . . . I wonder if I'll ever get credit for it, in Heaven, perhaps. And anyway, if he'd cried, I'd have got the blame, because I'm older and should know better. Anne never gets the blame if she upsets *me*. I'm pig in the middle. One day I shall be grown up. I shall be as old as Anne, and then as old as Emily and get married, and then as old as my mother with children and then as old as Granny Burridge, and then I shall die like Grandad Burridge and Granny Filkins. And Bertie. I'm eleven. Bertie would be thirteen. Anyway I didn't want Georgie's monkey face next to mine, he always looks funny in photographs. Georgie had to go to the other side to balance the picture. I suppose otherwise it would fall over or something. Silly way of putting it, balance, balance is for weight not pictures. He'll probably crack the lens. . . . Georgie spilt something down his front, I don't know what it was, my mother was ages trying to get it off so that it wouldn't show in the photograph. It would be more typical if it did. I hope this fly shows, but I don't suppose it will. My hands are folded, one on the other as I've been taught. I'm wearing a large hat. I'm looking, looking, looking at the camera. This picture will last for ever. But I shall die.

Whistle Down The Wind
Mary Hayley Bell

The village children are taught in their Sunday School that one day Jesus will return to the world. A criminal is on the run in the area, and 12-year-old Swallow finds a sick and hungry man in her father's barn whom she believes to be Jesus. In this scene in the barn she tells some of the local children about the man. Her sister, Brat, says that Swallow is rather bird-like, 'skimming low over ponds or flying with speed and grace'. She's also a capable, kind girl, who has looked after her brother and sister since their mother's death. . . . This novel was first published in 1958 and made into a very popular film in 1961; and later into a stage production.

SWALLOW. Can you keep a secret? A really big secret? You've got to hold up your hand and do the 'See this wet' routine:

> See this wet, see this dry,
> Cut my throat if I tell a lie . . . .

This is a great and fabulous secret known to none but those within these walls. You have to join a society to be allowed to know the secret, and all who know must swear never to divulge. Will you absolutely swear? If you ever breathe a word something ghastly will happen to you. . . . Alright. . . . That's Jesus. . . . We have proof. We were in here messing about. There was a sort of knock on the door and I opened it. He stood there smiling at us, and said, 'Knock on the door and it shall be opened unto you.' . . . And I said, 'Who are you?' and he stood staring round this place, not answering at once, and then suddenly said, rather loud: 'JESUS' . . . just like that. . . . His legs were all cut, and his boots and socks crammed with mud and he kind of lurched. I asked Him if I should get someone and He said 'Don't tell them till I've recovered'. . . . He's ill . . . too ill to talk. He's been asleep for six hours! . . . In the daytime! . . . The grown-ups may not believe . . . suppose they try and take Him away . . . after all they did last time. . . . But we can have a gigantic meeting, we can tell them all . . . swear them all to secrecy. There's hundreds of children around here and every child knows other children. We can bring them a few at a time to see Him and hear His words. Little by little we can spread the news to children all over the country that the first people to know Jesus has come back will be the children. And . . . if the grown-ups try to take Him away again, we'll defend Him. . . . Hundreds of us!

The Adoption Papers
Jackie Kay

This is a play in verse about a black girl's adoption by a white Scottish couple, from three viewpoints: the mother, the birth mother and the daughter. In this sequence the daughter is at first about 8 years old, and after the pause, shown by . . . . . . to denote the passing of time, about 12 years old. The settings are in a primary school playground and a school classroom in Glasgow. Originally adapted for radio in 1991, the work can be imaginatively presented as live theatre, and there are other sections equally possible as solo scenes.

DAUGHTER. I chase his *Sambo Sambo* all the way from
 the school gate.
A fistful of anorak – What did you call me? Say that
 again.
Sam-bo. He plays the word like a bouncing ball
but his eyes move fast as ping pong.
I shove him up against the wall,
say that again you wee shite. *Sambo, sambo*, he's crying
 now

I knee him in the balls. What was that?
My fist is steel; I punch and punch his gut.
Sorry I didn't hear you? His tears drip like wax.
Nothing he heaves *I didn't say nothing*.
I let him go. He is a rat running. He turns
and shouts *Dirty Darkie* I chase him again.
Blond hairs in my hand. Excuse me!
This teacher from primary 7 stops us.
Names? I'll report you to the headmaster tomorrow.
But Miss. Save it for Mr Thompson she says

26

My teacher's face cracks into a thin smile
Her long nails scratch the note well well
I see you were fighting yesterday, again.
In a few years' time you'll be a juvenile delinquent.
Do you know what that is? Look it up in the dictionary.
She spells each letter with slow pleasure.
Read it out to the class.
Thug. Vandal. Hooligan. Speak up. Have you lost your
    tongue?

. . . . . .

We're practising for the school show
I'm trying to do the Cha Cha and the Black Bottom
but I can't get the steps right
my right foot's left and my left foot's right
my teacher shouts from the bottom
of the class Come on, show

us what you can do I thought
you people had it in your blood.
My skin is hot as burning coal
like that time she said Darkies are like coal
in front of the whole class – my blood
what does she mean? I thought

she'd stopped all that after the last time
my dad talked to her on parents' night
the other kids are all right till she starts;
my feet step out of time, my heart starts
to miss beats like when I can't sleep at night –
What Is In My Blood? The bell rings, it is time.

Invisible Friends
Alan Ayckbourn

Lucy is an ordinary young teenager, absolutely fed up with her family who are too pre-occupied with their own lives to bother about her place in the school swimming team. In protest Lucy resorts to her childhood fantasy friend, Zara, who not only materializes in the play, but introduces her own ideal family and shows Lucy how to make HER family vanish.

Time: The present. In Lucy's house.

LUCY (*as she goes upstairs, to audience*). Come with me, if you will. Upstairs. If you listen very carefully you can just hear the distant sounds of the greater spotted Grisly Gary, my unbelievably talkative brother. Grisly Gary is doing a building course at the technical college, training to be a bucket. (*She reaches the door of* GARY's *room. The music is louder now.*) Here we go. I'll just have a quiet word with him. Cover your ears.

LUCY *opens* GARY's *door. The heavy-metal music comes up to a deafening level.* LUCY, *when she speaks, is quite inaudible.* GARY, *lying on the bed with his eyes closed, fails to notice her at all.*

(*Mouthing, swiftly.*) Hallo, Grisly. It's your loving sister, Lucy. Just to tell you I've been picked for the school swimming team. Thought you'd like to know. Bye, Grisly. (LUCY *closes the door again. The music goes down to a lower level.*) I enjoyed that chat. (*She opens the door of her own room and goes inside.*) This is my room. No one's allowed in here, except me. I'm a very tidy sort
28

of person. Which is a bit extraordinary in this house. I think I must be a freak. I actually like to know where I've put my things. This is my bed. That's my desk. And up there on the shelf. Those are my special, most favourite books. (*The music pounds through the wall.*) Actually, one of the reasons I keep it tidy is because my very, very best friend, Zara, also likes things tidy. Oh yes, I ought to explain to you about Zara. You may have heard my mum talking about my invisible friend. Do you remember? Well, that's my invisible friend, Zara. (*Introducing her.*) This is Zara. I want you to meet Zara. Zara say hallo. That's it. Will you say hallo to Zara, my invisible friend? I invented Zara – oh, years ago – when I was seven or eight. Just for fun. I think I was ill at that time and wasn't allowed to play with any of my real friends, so I made up Zara. She's my special friend that no one can see except me. Of course, I can't really see her either. Not really. Although sometimes I . . . . It's almost as if I could see her, sometimes. If I concentrate very hard it's like I can just glimpse her out of the corner of my eye. (*She is thoughtful for a second.*) Still. Anyway. I've kept Zara for years and years. Until they all started saying I was much too old for that sort of thing and got worried and started talking about sending for a doctor. So then I didn't take her round with me quite so much after that. But she's still here. And when I feel really sad and depressed like I do today, then I sit and talk to Zara. Zara always understands. Zara always listens. She's special. Aren't you, Zara? (*She listens to* ZARA. *Pause.*) Oh, Zara, did I tell you I've been picked for the school swimming team? Isn't that exciting? Yes. Thank you. I'm glad you're excited, too. Good. (*Pause. Shouting.*) IF ANYONE IS INTERESTED AT ALL, I WAS PICKED FOR THE SCHOOL SWIMMING TEAM TODAY. WHAT ABOUT THAT, FOLKS? (*She

29

listens. No reply.) Great. Thanks for your support, everyone. (*Tearful.*) They might at least . . . They could have at least . . . Oh, Zara . . . I know you're always here, but sometimes I get so . . . lonely . . .

She sits on her bed, sad, angry and frustrated.

The Burston Drum
Ellen Dryden (with lyrics by Don Taylor)

This musical play is based on the true story of what came to be known as the 'Longest Strike in History'. On 1 April 1914 in the village of Burston, near Diss, Norfolk, a group of children went on strike to protest at the unfair dismissal of their teachers, Kitty and Tom Higdon. These two dedicated teachers believed that village children from poor working families deserved a better education and chance in life. As they had previously experienced, the School Managers and Councillors were against their ideals, but the village children and their parents fought on their behalf. The Burston Rebellion continued until 1939, the strike school meeting at first in temporary buildings and from 1917 in a more permanent one. In this scene Violet Potter, leader of the children, 13 years old, lively, staunch and intelligent talks to the pupils. She holds a paper in her hand. The scene is in a darkened schoolroom, lit by the children's torches and lanterns.

VIOLET. Ssh. We don't want them to know we're in here. We'll all have to go home in a minute or they'll come looking for us. Keep away from the windows with those torches. . . . Now you heard what Mr Durbridge said at the meeting out on the Green. They've sacked our teachers. The School Board man is coming to tell them to get out of this school by the first of April. That's tomorrow!! They won't even let them stay till the summer holidays! That means they've got to get all their things out of here by tomorrow. The Mistress has asked us if we'll help her carry her own things back to the schoolhouse and load up the cart. . . . Quiet! Listen to me. . . . We can do more than help them load up and leave. Now. Do you want the Governess and

31

Mr Higdon to go? (*There's a loud 'No'.*) SSSssshhhh! (*They whisper 'No'.*) Will you do ANYTHING to help them to stay? (*Everyone whispers 'Yes!!'.*) Well then. You heard what Mr Durbridge said to our Mums and Dads. They don't want them to go either and they're going to do all they can to keep them here. But nobody can do as much as we can. . . . (*Replying to a reaction.*) No – I know they won't listen to us. And we needn't listen to THEM. What's the good of them getting a new teacher and letting the school carry on without Mr and Mrs Higdon if WE'RE not here! If we don't come, there's no school! . . . Marjorie and I have got a list here, and we want you all to sign it, to say that you won't come to school at all if they take our teachers. Do you want to sign it? (*Everyone does and while* MARJORIE *collects the signatures* VIOLET *writes on the blackboard which faces away from the audience, the sentences TODAY IS MARCH* 31st 1914. *TOMORROW WE ARE GOING ON STRIKE.*) So instead of coming to school tomorrow we all meet on the Green. If they won't listen when we talk to them we'll SHOW them what we mean. They'll hear us tomorrow all right!

Tokens of Affection
Maureen Lawrence

*The pupils at a centre for violent and majadjusted adolescent girls
are in a state of unrest, with the members of staff and each other.
Liane is described as 'school-phobic, not a real nasty . . . no saint,
but at least she's little'. She trades on her smallness, is whiny, can
be sly, manipulative, a sneak. At present one arm is in a sling.
Having fallen out with the other girls, Liane here attempts to get
the new girl, Andrea, on to her side.*

Time: The present. A room in the centre, Northern England.

ANDREA *prowls. She finds the craft knife, tests the blade and
with one or two swift strokes mutilates* KELLY's *sewing. She
is still holding the knife when* LIANE *enters.*

LIANE (*involuntarily*). Debbie nicked that knife off Mrs
Leiver. It goes in the cupboard. Now she's come, she'll
try and get Kelly back. I'll be on my own again. I never
had a mate of my own. Even at home. They all pick on
me. It's because I look like my Dad. When they sent me
away to that school, my Mother never meant for me to come
back. She burned my bed. She took it out in the yard and
burned everything. You can see where she did it – the bits
that wouldn't burn just got left there. I said: you expect
me to fucking sleep in the yard on a bunch of burnt rags
and she hit me across the mouth. I don't care. I lie on the
sofa and watch telly all night till it wakes me up with that
whining it makes. (*Pause.*) Debbie won't touch you: you're
big. You've got brothers. Do you talk to your brothers? My
Mam gets like, paralysed. Stiff as a board. We have to lug
her onto the lavatory, me and our June. It was all right here
without Debbie. Better than stopping in the house. Are you

miserable? Why don't you say nothing? My Mother says I never stop yapping. How do you stop yourself yapping? My Mother says she's going to put tape on my lips. Andrea? It's miles better here than at school. I'm never going back to no school. If them in schools knew what it was like when you get expelled they'd all be getting expelled. Schools would be empty. Teachers would be out of work. You won't get me nowhere near. You think when you hear that word expelled it means something terrible, but it's a big con. Me, first of all I had a holiday for seven weeks and then I ended up in this place. Our June, that's my sister, the one that's pregnant, our June says: trust you to fall on your feet. My Mother says: better to fall on your feet, our June, than flat on your back with your legs wide open. Andrea? Can you hear me? If Debbie gets Kelly back, you could ask Mrs Rushworth if you could be with me? Andrea?

Bleak House
Charles Dickens

Amongst the many characters involved in a complex legal case of wills and trusts is the motherless Esther Summerson, ward of Mr Jarndyce. He has arranged for another orphan girl, Charlotte Neckett . . . Charley . . . to be Esther's maid. Charley is about 13, 'childish in figure, but shrewd and older-looking in the face, – pretty-faced, too – a hard-working mother to her small brother and sister'.
 Setting: Esther's Rooms.
 Time: The nineteenth century.

CHARLEY. If you please Miss, I am Charley . . . if you please, miss, I'm your maid . . . if you please Miss, I'm a present to you, with Mr Jarndyce's love. And O, Miss . . . (*Tears starting down her cheeks.*) . . . Tom's at school, if you please, and learning so good! And little Emma, she's with Mrs Blinder, Miss, a being took such care of! And Tom, he would have been at school . . . and Emma, she would have been left with Mrs Blinder . . . and me, I should have been here . . . all a deal sooner, Miss; only Mr Jarndyce thought that Tom and Emma and me had better get a little used to parting first, we was so small. Don't cry, if you please, Miss! Though I know you can't help it, Miss, and nor I can't help it. And if you please, Miss, Mr Jarndyce's love, and he thinks you'll like to teach me now and then. And, if you please, Tom and Emma and me is to see each other once a month, and I'm so happy and so thankful, Miss, and I'll try to be such a good maid. . . . And I'll never forget who did all this. I never will. Nor Tom won't. Nor yet Emma. It was all you, Miss. I know Mr Jarndyce helped too, Miss, but it was all done for the love of you, and that you might be my mistress. If you please, Miss, I am a little present with his love, and it was all done for the love of you. Me and Tom was to be sure to remember it. . . . Oh, don't cry if you please, Miss . . . but I can't help it neither. . . . (*And she cries.*)

Dreams of Anne Frank
Bernard Kops

The events in this version of Anne Frank's life are created atmospherically, with the minimum of scenery and furniture. Music and a fluidity of action, suggest the dreams and imaginings of the 13-year-old Jewish girl. This is the opening of the play, linking two scenes together.

Time: 1942, in Amsterdam, Holland, during the Second World War.

ANNE. Morning star, evening star, yellow star. Amsterdam. 1942. The German army occupies Holland. They have applied terrible rules that we must obey. Rules for Jews. That applies to me. 'Jews must wear a yellow star. Jews cannot go on trains. Jews must not drive. Jews cannot go shopping, except between three and five. Jews must only patronise Jewish shops.' We cannot go to the cinema, play tennis, go swimming. I cannot even go to the theatre. And now for the most frightening thing of all. They are beginning to round Jews up and take us away. Away from our homes, our beloved Amsterdam. A few days ago I celebrated my thirteenth birthday. My parents gave me this diary. It is my most precious possession. Yesterday I was just an ordinary girl living in Amsterdam. Today I am forced to wear this by our Nazi conquerors. Morning star, evening star, yellow star.

Where are we going to hide? . . . Will we be alright? . . . What do I leave behind? What can I take? . . . (*Gets her satchel as she hears the answer 'Absolute essentials'.*) Essentials. My school satchel. I'm going to cram it full. Hair curlers . . . . Handkerchiefs. School books. Film star

37

photographs. Joan Crawford. Bette Davis. Deanna Durbin. Mickey Rooney. Comb. Letters. Thousands of pencils. Elastic bands. My best book. *Emil and the Detectives*. Five pens. (*She smells a little bottle.*) Nice scent. Oh yes! Mustn't forget my new diary. Have you seen it? . . . We're going into hiding. Going into hiding. (*The others, the family, are all busy packing.*) Four days later. It was Thursday the 9th of July. I shall never forget that morning. It was raining. Imagine leaving your house, maybe forever. . . . Goodbye, house. . . . We'll always remember you. . . . Thank you for everything. My brain is at a fairground, on the roller coaster. Up and down. Happy. Sad. Afraid. Excited. My emotions are racing. My imagination spilling over. After all, I am a creative artist. I'm going to be a writer when this war is over. (*She lingers as the others wait.*) Imagine leaving your house, forever. (*Starts to go, but stops. . . .*) Diary! Can't go without my diary. . . . Hello diary. . . . I shall write everything down. Everything. Thoughts. Events. Dreams. . . . I shall confide my secrets. Only to you.

National Velvet
Enid Bagnold

Against all odds 14-year-old Velvet Brown has won the Grand National, disguised as a jockey. Now, after the initial excitement, a film company want her to appear in a film with her prize-winning horse, the Piebald. Velvet is an inspired lover of horses. She is described as 'delicate and spiny . . . feather-weight . . . with short pale hair, large protruding teeth, a sweet smile and a mouth full of metal'. Her trainer, Mi, when looking closely to decide if she could pass as a boy, declared her chest to be 'flat as a pancake'.

Setting: The Brown family's cottage living room.

Time: The Thirties.

VELVET. Wants the horse? Can't have the horse. (*Firmly.*) Piebald on the films! He seems to forget! (*Proudly.*) That THAT'S the horse that won the National. . . . I'll go. It won't be half bad for us all to go and see me doing things on the curtain an' the band playing an' us sitting looking. But the Piebald! He doesn't know, he wouldn't know. He's out there in that field, steady and safe. He believes in me. I wouldn't let him in for a thing he couldn't understand. He's not like a human. He doesn't know how to be funny . . . (*Tears coming now.*) . . . and he SHAN'T LEARN! . . . (*Still sobbing.*) I've read about horses . . . horses that has won . . . an' they write about them nobly as though they were statues . . . . Now how can you write about a horse nobly if it goes on the films? . . . I don't mean in the papers . . . not in the papers . . . (*Gulping, pulling herself together.*) Mother lights the fire with those! In books! Big books! Roll-of-Honour Books where they put down the winners and call them the Immortal Manifesto. . . . Now, how can they call him the Immortal Piebald if he goes on the films?! (*Hysterical*.) ME! That's nothing! I'm nothing! If you could see what he did for me! . . . an' when I asked him he burst himself more! . . . an' when I asked him again he doubled it! He tried near to death, he did. . . . I'd sooner have that horse happy than . . . than go to heaven!

Daisy Pulls It Off
Denise Deegan

*This comedy is a pastiche of the popular schoolgirl stories of the
Twenties by writers like Angela Brazil and Ethel Talbot. But it
must not be 'sent up' or over-acted in such a way as to spoil its
sincerity and heart. It tells the story of Daisy Meredith, a poor
Elementary School girl who wins a scholarship to Grangewood
School for Young Ladies. This speech is at the very start of the play.
The letter could be placed on the floor, ready for Daisy to find.*
    Time: 1927.

DAISY (*to the audience*). Daisy Meredith, daredevil, tom-
boy, possessed of a brilliant mind, exuberant, quick-witted,
fond of practical jokes, honourable, honest, courageous,
straight in all things and . . . an Elementary School pupil.
Father – dead. Mother – a former opera singer who struggles
to keep a home together for herself, Daisy, and Daisy's
brothers – Dick, Douglas, Daniel and Duncan in a small
terraced house in London's East End, by giving music
lessons to private pupils. Daisy has recently taken an
exam which will, if she succeeds in passing it, enable
her to gain a place as the first ever scholarship pupil
at Grangewood Girls School, one of the most famous
educational establishments in the country. If, however,
she fails the exam, she must leave her Elementary School
at the end of the year and take up some form of ill-paid
menial work to which she is little suited. Thank you. . . .
(*To herself.*) I do wish the postman would hurry and bring
the letter containing the exam results – but it isn't even
eight o'clock yet. I must win the scholarship, I so want
to go to Grangewood. How topping it would be to learn

41

Latin and Greek, to play hockey on their famous pitch, to make friends with all those jolly girls and have midnight feasts and get into fearful scrapes just like they do in books. I should miss Mother and Dick, Douglas, Daniel and Duncan of course . . . and all my chums at Elementary School. But I must win the scholarship for the sake of others as well as for myself, for if I, the first scholarship pupil at Grangewood, make a success of the scheme, Grangewood will open its doors to other Elementary School pupils, as poor as myself. . . . (*The letter arrives.*) Mother! Oh, Mother, I'm through! I've got the scholarship, I can go to Grangewood. . . . (MOTHER *enters and helps* DAISY *get into her uniform.*) I hope I make a success of it. I'll have a good education, pass all my exams and then, when I leave, find a job as a teacher in an Elementary School and perhaps I'll earn enough money to buy you the country cottage you've always wanted, and to pay for Dick, Douglas, Daniel and Duncan's education if they haven't won a scholarship by then. . . . (*To the audience.*) The summer holidays passed all too slowly, for Daisy, that is, until the time came to say goodbye to those she loved best. . . . Write often, Mother, I'll be dying to know what you're all doing, and any news you may hear of my old school pals. (*Hearing a whistle off.*) We're off – oh, Mother. See you at the end of term.

All Things Nice
Sharman Macdonald

Although dominated by her much sharper, more knowing, street-wise friend, Linda, Moira is more sensitively aware of her own developing sexuality and growing-up. Influenced by Linda, Moira is persuaded to report and give evidence against a man the two girls see exposing himself one day. When the man subsequently commits suicide, Linda grows uneasy.

The setting: In front of a mirror, just before the court case. The play uses Scottish dialect, but may be set anywhere in Britain.

Time: The present.

MOIRA *is standing at the mirror with her glasses on.*

LINDA. Take those (glasses) off. Take them off. (MOIRA *turns to look at her.*) All right. At least wear socks. Take your stockings off. Go on, Moira. A nice white pair of socks. (MOIRA *stands there.*) What are you going to say? At least warn me. Prepare me. I'll tell the truth. I didn't see him. Not then. Not after school. It was him. It was him all right. As had been doing it. But he wasn't doing it then. Not right then. Or maybe he was. It was getting dark. I don't know what I saw. What are you going to say? Moira? We've been friends a long time. We shared a play-pen together. My God. Moira. Here. (*She holds out a blue velvet Alice band.*) Look at this. I've brought you this. Don't tell me what you're going to say. Remember we used to play hairdressers. Remember you cut my hair off and I wanted you to, and mum nearly killed us and she plaited up my hair and she put it in a box. How she cried. Eh, Moira? She has it yet. And my teeth. She collected all my teeth one by one as they fell out. The Tooth Fairy never visited our house. She put them in the

43

box too. My mum. She gives me the shivers. My mum. She's a witch. My mum. All she has to do. I do something she doesn't like. She takes out one of my teeth and sticks a pin in it. She does. Takes it out of the walnut box and jabs a pin right in. I swear she does. I get awful toothache sometimes. It's our mothers make us what we are. I was a very nice person when I was born. She'll not like me being a liar. Don't you make me a liar, Moira. Please. Sit down. I'll make you look nice. Moira. I'll brush your hair for you. She's so proud of me, my mum. Remember how we used to play? Moira. . . .

She brushes MOIRA's *hair. Gently. Puts in the Alice band.*

The Two Noble Kinsmen
John Fletcher and William Shakespeare

*This play is loosely based on Chaucer's fourteenth-century 'The
Knight's Tale' from* The Canterbury Tales, *which in its turn
derives from the Italian of Boccaccio. The story of the shifting
fortunes of two Knights, Arcite and Palamon who have the
misfortune to love the same woman, has the addition to the
plot of the Gaoler's Daughter. This young girl falls madly in
love with the imprisoned Palamon, and her distress makes her
mad; this madness is cured by a lower-class suitor pretending to
be Palamon. The play was probably written in about 1613.*

Enter GAOLER's DAUGHTER *alone.*

DAUGHTER.
Why should I love this gentleman? 'Tis odds
He never will affect me; I am base,
My father the mean keeper of his prison,
And he a prince. To marry him is hopeless;
To be his whore is witless. Out upon't!
What pushes are we wenches driven to
When fifteen once has found us! First I saw him;
I, seeing, thought he was a goodly man;
He has as much to please a woman in him –
If he please to bestow it so – as ever
These eyes yet looked on. Next, I pitied him,
And so would any young wench, o' my conscience,
That ever dreamed, or vowed her maidenhead
To a young handsome man. Then I loved him,
Extremely loved him, infinitely loved him;
And yet he had a cousin, fair as he too;
But in my heart was Palamon, and there,

Lord, what a coil he keeps! To hear him
Sing in an evening, what a heaven it is!
And yet his songs are sad ones. Fairer spoken
Was never gentleman; when I come in
To bring him water in a morning, first
He bows his noble body, then salutes me, thus:
'Fair, gentle maid, good morrow; may thy goodness
Get thee a happy husband.' Once he kissed me;
I loved my lips the better ten days after –
Would he would do so every day! He grieves much,
And me as much to see his misery.
What should I do to make him know I love him?
For I would fain enjoy him. Say I ventured
To see him free? What says the law then? Thus much
For law or kindred! I will do it;
And this night, or tomorrow, he shall love me.

Exit.

When We Are Married
J B Priestley

Three respectable couples, 'pillars of society', were married by the same parson 25 years ago and have met together to celebrate their Silver Weddings. The party is taking place in the home of Alderman and Mrs Helliwell, a solid Victorian house in Clecklewyke, in the West Riding of Yorkshire. Gerald Forbes, the new young organist has called (he is courting Councillor Parker's niece) and been ushered into the sitting-room by Ruby Birtle, a girl of about 15, 'a young slavey of the period, who looks as if her hair has just gone up'. She talks in a marked West Riding dialect.

Time: September 1908.

RUBY. You'll have to wait, 'cos they haven't finished their tea. . . . (*Approaching* GERALD, *confidentially.*) It's a do. . . . A do. Y'know, they've company. (*Going closer.*) They're having roast pork, stand pie, salmon and salad, trifle, two kinds o' jellies, lemon-cheese tarts, jam tarts, swiss tarts, sponge cake, walnut cake, chocolate roll, and a pound cake kept from last Christmas. . . . (*Seriously.*) . . . No, that's not all. There's white bread, brown bread, currant tea-cake, one o' them big curd tarts from Gregory's and a lot o' cheese. . . . (*Very confidentially.*) AND a little brown jug. . . . You know what that is, don't you? DON'T YOU? (*Laughs.*) Well, I never did! A little brown jug's a drop o' rum for your tea. They're getting right lively on it. (*Coolly.*) But you don't come from round here, do you? . . . I come from near Rotherham. Me father works in t'pit, and so does our Frank and our Wilfred. (*Bell sounds, distant again.*) I know. It's for me. Let her wait. She's run me off

47

me legs today. And Mrs Northrop's in t'kitchen – she can do a bit for a change. . . . There's seven of 'em at it in t'dining-room – Alderman Helliwell and Missus, of course – then Councillor Albert Parker and Mrs Parker, and Mr Herbert Soppitt and Mrs Soppitt – and, of course, Miss Holmes . . . but she's stopped eating. (*She giggles.*) You're courting her aren't you? . . . (*Coolly.*) Oh – I saw you both – the other night, near Cleckley Woods. I was out meself with our milkman's lad. . . . Now don't look like that, I won't tell on you. . . . (*She sees him produce a shilling.*) But I'd like that shilling. . . . D'you want to see her? I told you she's finished eating. She can't put it away like some of 'em. You think they'd been pined for a month – way they're going at it! I'll tell her . . . (*Moves to go, then turns back.*) She'd better come round that way – through t'green-house – Oh, by the way, my name's Ruby Birtle.

Brand
Henrik Ibsen

Brand, the chief character in this verse-play is a discontented and uncompromising priest who sets off on an 'all or nothing' quest of the conscience with the sole objective of discovering how to be 'True to Thyself'. Gerd is a wild gypsy-girl of 15 who is similar to Brand in that she is the product of a loveless marriage and as a result has come to fear and distrust love as Brand has. In this scene Gerd comes rushing down from the mountains to direct Brand to the Church of Ice, a symbol of the rejection of all his past beliefs and ultimately the destination of his death. The play was written in 1865.

GERD *runs down the path and stops outside the garden gate.*

GERD (*claps her hands and shouts gleefully*). Have you
    heard? The parson's flown away!
  The trolls and demons are swarming out of the hillsides,
  Black and ugly. Big ones, small ones – oh!
  How sharply they can strike! They nearly
  Tore my eye out. They've taken half my soul.
  But I can manage with what's left. . . .

  My hawk swept down the mountainside
  From Black Peak. Bridled, saddled, wild and angry,
  Hissing down the evening wind. And on his back
  A man rode. The priest, it was the priest!
  The village church stands empty, locked and barred.
  It's time is up; it's ugly.
  My church's time has come now. There stands my priest,
  Big and strong, in his white cloak woven of ice.
  Come along with me! . . .

Can you see the thousand trolls
The village priest drowned in the sea?
That grave can't hold them; they're groping their way
    ashore,
Cold and slimy. Look at the troll children!
They're only skin-dead; see how they grin
As they push up the rocks that pinned them down. . . .

Listen! Can you hear that one laughing
As he sits astride the crosspoint where the road
Swings up to the moor, writing down in his book
The name of every soul that passes? He has them all.
The old church stands empty, locked and barred.
The priest flew away on the hawk's back.

*She leaps over the gate and disappears among the rocks.
Silence.*

Translated by Michael Meyer

Brother in the Land
Robert Swindells

There has been a nuclear holocaust. Some people in a town in Northern England have survived. Amongst them are Danny, Kim and her sister Maureen, who is expecting a child. . . . One of the many fears is that the soil is seriously contaminated. In this scene, Kim rushes in to the refectory, carrying a misshapen swede. She has become quite wild as she approaches Danny. (Adapted from the novel.)

KIM. See this, Danny Lodge? D'you know what this is, eh? Well, I'll tell you. It's a swede, but it's not your ordinary, everyday swede. Oh, no. This is an Hiroshima swede, Danny-boy, and we also do Hiroshima turnips, Hiroshima beans, Hiroshima spuds and Hiroshima rotten cabbage. Oh yes, and I nearly forgot. Hiroshima babies. We can do you a nice Hiroshima baby if you like. . . . The first of many! . . . (*Rushes screaming from the room . . . to an old broken down shed . . . as DANNY approaches her.*) . . . I'm sorry I shouted at you. I don't know why I did it. I'll never be able to go in that refectory again and I don't know how I'll face the others in the hut tonight. They were all there. . . . D'you think they'll understand? I wish they would, because, you don't know what it's like, Danny. There's twenty-nine of them in my hut. Twenty-nine, and all they ever say to me is you are looking after that sister of yours, aren't you? We can't have anything happening to her and the baby now, can we? What do you hope it will be, a boy or a girl? And all the time I'm trying to forget about the rotten baby so I can get some sleep at night. Last time somebody asked me that last one I said, yes, I hope it's a boy or a girl, but they didn't get it, they still kept on. . . . Can you tell me why you haven't been thinking about it all these weeks as I have? Why you're pestering me to marry you so we can make a monster too? . . . There weren't many normal babies in Hiroshima . . . not even with the best medical attention in the world. And that was nothing, one tiny bomb. . . . So you go on hoping if you can, only don't expect me to push it to the back of my mind and rush off and marry you and live happily ever after. . . . I know there's nothing anybody can do. That's the awful part of it. Waiting. I've been doing nothing else for weeks and I'm tired and scared and fed up. Oh, Danny! What's going to happen to us all? How's it going to end, Danny?

A Boston Story
Ronald Gow (from the novel by Henry James)

Nora Lambert is 16 years old and the adopted daughter of a young middle-aged man, Roger Lawrence. She has just left school and is now coming to take up her place in his home outside Boston, where he has had a wing built for her. She is attractive, a little tomboyish, lively and serious too. It is Christmas Eve in the Library, 1877, and Nora has been making decorations. Roger is smoking his pipe by the fire.

NORA (*at the window*). Yes. It is still snowing. It's all white outside. And very silent. It makes me feel that you and I are alone in the world. . . . (*Reacting to a remark he makes.*) . . . I'm not YOUR little girl. . . . No, Roger, I'm not. I'm no one's little girl. Do you think I can't remember. . . . (*Sits on the floor beside him.*) Sometimes I'm frightened. . . . Roger – suppose I only exist in your mind. That I'm not a person at all. That I'm nobody. . . . You told me that a man called Plato said we only existed in other people's minds. . . . Oh well, Bishop Berkeley, then. . . . (*Intensely.*) This is just the sort of night to talk about these things. I mean – about life and death – and who are we? Who am I? And who are you? . . . I am like something that you have made up in a fairy-tale. A princess. That's what I feel like. The truth is that I'm just a poor creature without a friend – even without a penny. And yet here I am – sitting by a blazing fire – warm and comfortable. Outside the snow is so deep that it's burying the stone walls. I shall wake up in the morning and say how beautiful it is. But suppose I were in it. Wandering and begging for my food. I might have

53

been. Should I think it beautiful then? Do you know, I think I should like to try. . . . I'd be a real person. . . . I would snap my fingers at your Bishop Berkeley and I would say 'Look, I'm real, I'm myself!' I want to feel how little that is, and who I really am. . . . NO! I don't belong to you! I want to be my own father's daughter. And my mother's too. I haven't spoken of them before. You must please let me tonight. You must talk to me about my father. Was he wicked? You never mentioned his name. He can do no harm, now he's dead, can he? We oughtn't to despise him – forget him altogether? Ought we? . . . I can remember that he took his own life . . . in that hotel in New York. . . . (*She looks into fire.*) There were some palms and a big staircase. . . . If ever I go back to New York I shall go and look for it. . . . Because it's the only home I can remember. . . . Tell me – wasn't he wonderfully handsome? . . . (ROGER *agrees.*) He used to play the piano and there was a great deal of singing. My mother used to sing, I'm sure. I can't remember her. . . . Poor dead things! Well, so much for the past. . . . Do you know, girls at school were always talking about their homes, and their fathers and their mothers. They seemed so much more real than I did. . . . Oh, you'd be surprised how girls talk, Roger. I never used to say very much. . . . (*Moving behind his chair.*) My future is fixed. With you. Isn't it? (*Hands on his shoulders.*) Roger – you shall never repent. I shall learn everything you order me to learn. I shall be everything you want me to be. (*Kisses him gravely, then turns away.*) Oh, how I wish I were pretty! . . . If you're satisfied, I suppose I am. It looks hopeless to me.

17+

Male and Female

Candida
Bernard Shaw

The setting is the sitting-room/study of St Dominic's Vicarage in North East London in 1894. Eugene Marchbanks is a strange shy young man of 18, over-romantic perhaps, and poetic, his character not yet formed. He has just announced to James Morell, the vicar, his love for Morell's attractive, lovable 33-year-old wife, Candida. Having likened the vicar to King David whose 'wife despised him in her heart' Marchbanks has been ordered to leave the house at once.

Note: The text follows Shaw's dictates in matters of spelling and punctuation.

MARCHBANKS (*shrinking back against the couch*). Let me alone. Dont touch me. (MORELL *grasps him powerfully by the lapel of his coat: he cowers down on the sofa and screams passionately.*) Stop, Morell: if you strike me, I'll kill myself: I wont bear it. (*Almost in hysterics.*) Let me go. Take your hand away. (*On the sofa, gasping, but relieved by the withdrawal of Morell's hand.*) I'm not afraid of you: it's you who are afraid of me.

(MORELL *turns away contemptuously.* EUGENE *scrambles to his feet and follows him.*) You think because I shrink from being brutally handled – because (*with tears in his voice*) I can do nothing but cry with rage when I am met with violence – because I cant lift a heavy trunk down from the top of a cab like you – because I cant fight you for your wife as a drunken navvy would: all that makes you think I'm afraid of you. But youre wrong. If I havnt got what you call British pluck, I havnt British cowardice either: I'm not afraid of a clergyman's ideas. I'll fight your ideas. I'll rescue her from

57

her slavery to them. I'll pit my own ideas against them. You are driving me out of the house because you darent let her choose between your ideas and mine. You are afraid to let me see her again. (MORELL, *angered, turns suddenly on him. He flies to the door in involuntary dread*.) Let me alone, I say I'm going. Tell her what I said; and how you were strong and manly, and shook me as a terrier shakes a rat; and how I shrank and was terrified; and how you called me a snivelling little whelp and put me out of the house. If you dont tell her, I will: I'll write to her. (*with lyric rapture*) Because she will understand me, and know that I understand her. If you keep back one word of it from her – if you are not ready to lay the truth at her feet as I am – then you will know to the end of your days that she really belongs to me and not to you. Goodbye. (*going*) Goodbye, Mr Clergyman.

Five Finger Exercise
Peter Shaffer

Walter, a young German, described as 'secret, precise but not priggish' is in England to tutor 14-year-old Pamela Harrington in languages. His presence has a compelling and significant effect on each member of the family. In this scene he attempts to get through to Clive who is 19 and in a depressed and nervous state.

Setting: The Harrington's weekend cottage in Suffolk.

Time: The late 1950's.

WALTER (*he closes the door and stands behind the armchair*). Clive? What's the matter? Are you all right? Why are you sitting in the dark? I've been talking to your father. He thinks you hate him. (CLIVE *does not appear to hear.*) Clive, listen to me. The Kings of Egypt were gods. Everything they did was right, everything they said was true, everyone they loved became important. And when they died, they grew faces of gold. You must try to forgive your parents for being average and wrong when you worshipped them once. Why are you so afraid? (*He moves down* R *of* CLIVE.) Is it – because you have no girlfriend? (*He sits on the stool,* R *of* CLIVE.) Oh, you are so silly. Silly. Do you think sex will change you? Put you into a different world, where everything will mean more to you? I thought so, too, once. I thought it would change me into a man so my father could never touch me again. I didn't know exactly what it would be like, but I thought it would burn me and bring me terrible pain. But afterwards, I'd be strong and very wise. There was a girl in Muhlbach. She worked in her mother's grocery shop. One night I had a few drinks

59

and, just for a joke, I broke into her bedroom through the window. I stayed with her all night. And I entered heaven. I really did. Between her arms was the only place in the world that mattered. When daylight came, I felt I had changed for ever. A little later I got up. I looked round, but the room was exactly the same. This was incomprehensible. It should have been so huge now – filled with air. But it seemed very small and stuffy and outside it was raining. I suppose I had thought, 'Now it will never rain again,' because rain depresses me, and I was now a man and could not be depressed. I remember, I hated the soap for lying there in the dish just as it had done the night before. I watched her putting on her clothes. I thought: 'We're tied together now by an invisible thread.' And then she said: 'It's nine o'clock: I must be off' – and went downstairs to open the shop. Then I looked into the mirror: at least my eyes would be different. (*Ironically.*) They were a little red, yes – but I was exactly the same – still a boy. Rain was still here. And all the problems of yesterday were still waiting. (*He pauses and puts his hand on* CLIVE's *arm.*) Sex by itself is nothing, believe me. Just like breathing – only important when it goes wrong. And Clive, this only happens if you're afraid of it. What are you thinking? (*He pauses.*) Please talk to me.

Chains
Elizabeth Baker

It is 1911 *in Lily and Charley Wilson's sitting room at* 55 *Acacia Avenue, London. Charley is a very ordinary young city clerk in a very ordinary job, but he has been offered the chance to go to Australia and, despite opposition, wants to take that chance.*

CHARLEY. Let's have it out. You may as well know, all of you . . . it's quite true, I want to go. I want to do as Tennant's done, chuck everything, and try my luck in the Colonies. As soon as I had a fair start Lily would come out. . . . It's just that I'm sick of the office and the grind every week and no change! – nothing new, nothing happening. Why I haven't seen anything of the world. I just settled down to it – why? – just because other chaps do, because it's the right thing. I only live for Saturday. . . . Of course it must make a difference my being married. . . . But I'll tell you what, marriage shouldn't tie a man up as if he was a slave. I don't want to desert Lily – she's my wife and I'm proud of it – but because I'm married, am I never to strike out in anything? People like us are just cowards. We seize on the first soft job – and there we stick, like whipped dogs. We're afraid to ask for anything, afraid to ask for a rise even – we wait till it comes. And when the boss says he won't give you one – do we up and say 'Then I'll go somewhere where I can get more'? Not a bit of it! What's the good of sticking on here all our lives? Why shouldn't somebody risk something sometimes? We're all so jolly frightened – we've got no spunk – that's where the others get the hold óver us – we slog on day after day

61

and when they cut our wages down we take it as meek as Moses. We're not men, we're machines. Next week I've got my choice – either to take less money to keep my job or to chuck it and try something else. You say – everybody says – keep the job. I expect I shall – I'm a coward like all of you – but what I want to know is, why can't a man have a fit of restlessness and all that, without being thought a villain? . . . Don't cry, Lil, for heaven's sake! Can't any of you see my point – or won't you?

Hamp
John Wilson

Private Arthur Hamp is described as 24 years old, 'gormless, a pathetic figure to everyone but himself'. There is an appealing innocence in him; he can't believe that an ordinary young man from a Lancashire mill town should be taken so seriously by the army simply because he had walked away from battle. But court-martial and death were law for desertion at that time and Lieutenant Hargreaves, to whom Hamp is speaking in this scene, has the task of documenting the evidence, trying to discover what might have affected Hamp's morale, causing him to desert.

Setting: the Army Prison, on the Western Front, during the Battle of Passchendaele 1917.

HAMP. . . . Nothing I can think on, right off. I said to you about Willie, sir, didn't I? . . . Willie Bryson, sir. . . . About when we were hit, like, sir. When he were killed. . . . I were along with him at the time. . . . Well, what I mean, sir, you could say that's in my mind – same as you were asking. Like, I don't think as much about it now, but you wouldn't be telling a lie if you said to them it's in my mind. . . . Only it's more seeing than thinking. . . . The way it happened like. . . . I were talking to Willie at the time. Course I've seen plenty folk getting killed – same as you have – same as everybody. Hundreds. Thousands. Quick and slow. Weren't the first time neither that I saw somebody getting blown to bits. Bits of nothing, sir – you know what it's like. I've had to wipe and scrape bits off of me afore that an' all – the same as everybody else – it weren't the first time. Weren't even same as Willie were anything special to me. Maybe a bit, like, him belonging up our street, but

63

only for that, nothing special. He never had much time for me at home, Willie. I couldn't tell you what kind of – It were quick, of course. Never saw it quicker, never, not for nobody. Couldn't tell you what kind of shell it were. I were nobbut five-six yards away, like, and I were only bleeding – scratches – five-six yards from him – but Willie weren't nowhere – only all over me. Bits. Red and yellow. You know what it's like without me telling you. They had to give me a new uniform. (*Pause.*) Same as I were saying, sir – couldn't tell you what were special about it, but it's the God's truth it's in my mind, like, if that's what you want to know. Not as bad as it was for a while, but – I'm still seeing it, like, sir, that's what I mean. True, sir.

Not About Heroes
Stephen Macdonald

A play based on the friendship of poets Siegfried Sassoon and Wilfred Owen who met at Craiglockhart War Hospital for Nervous Disorders in Edinburgh in 1917, during the First World War. The playwright has linked their actual poems and letters with his own writing. Owen was 24, recovering from shell shock. He wrote of 'the pity of war' and in his older friend, Sassoon, disillusioned with all that war stood for, he found his hero.

Lights go up on WILFRED OWEN. *He is ablaze with excitement and gratitude, and replying to a letter from Siegfried Sassoon.*

OWEN. My *dear* Sassoon! When I had opened your envelope in a quiet corner of the Club staircase, I sat on the stairs and groaned a little, and then I went up and loosed off 'a gourd, a Gothic vacu-um' of a letter – which I put by, as you would recommend for such effusions, until I could think over the thing without *grame*. . . . I *thank* you; but not on this paper only, or in any writing. You gave – with what Christ, if he had known Latin and dealt in oxymoron – might have called Sinister Dexterity. I *imagined* you were entrusting me with some holy secret concerning yourself. But the contents of this envelope have not intensified my feelings for you by the least *gramme*. . . . You must know that since mid-September, when you still regarded me as a tiresome little knocker-at-your-door, I held you as *Keats* plus *Christ* plus my *Commanding Officer* plus *Christ* plus my *Father Confessor* plus *Amenophis IV* – in profile. What is all this – mathematically? In effect, it is this: that I *love you*, dispassionately, so much, so *very* much, dear fellow,

65

that the blasting little smile you wear on reading this can't hurt me in the least. . . . . If you consider what the above names have, severally, done for me, you will know what you are doing. And you have *fixed* my life, however short. You did not *light* me: I was always a mad comet; but you have fixed me. I spun around you, a satellite, for a month, but I shall swing out soon, a dark star in the orbit where you will blaze. Some day I must tell you how we sang, shouted, whistled and danced through the dark lanes of Colinton; and how we laughed till the meteors showered around us, and we fell calm under the winter stars . . . (*A pause for reflection*.) And some of us saw the pathway of the spirits for the first time. And – seeing that pathway so far above us – we praised God with louder whistling and knew we loved one another as no men love for long . . . I wish you were less undemonstrative! – for I have many adjectives with which to qualify myself. As it is, I can only say I am, Your proud friend, Owen.

Lights fade on OWEN.

Orphans
Lyle Kessler

The scene is set in the shabby, cluttered living room of an old row house in North Philadelphia. If Phillip at times seems retarded it is that his development has been arrested by the way his older brother, Treat, has kept him at home and organised their odd existence since their mother's death. Treat has brought home an older man, Harold, met out drinking, has stolen his brief-case, gagged him and bound him to a chair. In this scene Phillip is left alone with Harold, and is at the window, looking out.

Time: The 1980s.

PHILLIP. Here comes somebody! Here comes an old man with a cane, got a newspaper under his arm, a little brown bag . . . probably has some Squibb's Mineral Oil in that brown bag, maybe a jar of Planter's Peanut Butter and a loaf of Friehoffer's Bakery bread. Gonna make himself some nice thick peanut butter sandwiches. . . . You say something, Mister? You speaking to me? . . . You hungry? Maybe you're hungry, maybe that's it. You working up an appetite listening to me talk about those delicious peanut butter sandwiches that old man is gonna make? . . . Treat's gonna be home real soon now. Probably make you a tuna sandwich, Star Kist tuna and mayo on toast. How's that sound? . . . Mmmmmmmmmmm. I figured you'd like that. I've been eating Star Kist tuna for lunch for years now. I used to make myself peanut butter sandwiches, but I got sick of them. I like variety in my food. (*At window.*) Look at that, Mister! Two girls walking by . . . you're really missing something. (*Runs across room to other window.*) One's wearing real tight dungarees, the other's got on a skirt. I like

67

the one with them tight dungarees. Only thing is, Mister, there's a shoe out there now, a shoe staring me straight in the face, driving me crazy. (*Crosses to* HAROLD.) Listen Mister, if I climb out this window and bring back that shoe, you'll keep it to yourself, won't you? . . . 'Cause Treat has a hell of a temper, especially if he's crossed. He was in and out of the House of Detention when he was a kid. Him and me are brothers! (*Runs to window, stops, turns.*) Only thing is I ain't supposed to go out Mister, 'cause I have a terrible allergy, allergic to almost everything: plants, grass, trees, pollen. I almost died once! I went on over to Lincoln's restaurant, corner of Broad and Olney, with Treat . . . my face got red, tongue swelled up, I was gasping for breath. I got it Mister! I'll hold my breath so's I don't breathe in any of that deadly pollen. I can trust you, can't I, Mister? You're gonna keep your mouth shut, ain't you? . . . Okay. . . .

PHILLIP *takes a deep breath, wraps scarf round his face, climbs out . . . . During his short absence* HAROLD *manages to rock himself into a standing position and hop the chair to other side of room.* PHILLIP *returns through window with shoe. Closes window, unwraps scarf, takes a deep breath. Turns and sees* HAROLD. *Upset.*

What are you doing over there, Mister? . . . How did you get over there? . . . You shouldn't be over there. I don't think Treat is gonna like this. You're supposed to be sitting over here. Only thing is, I ain't supposed to touch you. I'm only supposed to watch you and see that everything is okay. I don't know what I'm gonna do now, Mister, Treat's gonna come home soon and ask how come you're over there, and I don't know what I'm gonna say!

The Vortex
Noël Coward

*Florence Lancaster is a well-known society beauty with many
lovers and enemies, who has put her social life before her husband
David, and pianist son, Nicky. Nicky's relationship with Bunty
Mainwaring has ended and he is taking drugs (a fact not yet
known to his mother) and is in a disturbed, distressed state.
He has come to her room late at night, determined to confront
her about her lifestyle. Although very much a 'period piece' and
seemingly over-dramatic, the scene must be played sincerely and
truthfully. Nicky Lancaster is 24, strained and white-faced, dressed
in pyjamas and dressing gown.*
Time: 1924.

NICKY. Look at me. . . . You've given me *nothing* all
my life – nothing that counts. . . . You forget what I've
seen tonight, Mother. . . . I've seen you make a vulgar,
disgusting scene in your own house, and on top of that
humiliate yourself before a boy half your age. The misery of
losing Bunty faded away when that happened – everything
is comparative after all. . . . You ran after him up the stairs
because your vanity wouldn't let you lose him – it isn't
that you love him – that would be easier – you never love
anyone, you only love them loving you – all your so-called
passion and temperament is false – your whole existence has
degenerated into an endless empty craving for admiration
and flattery – and then you say you've done no harm to
anybody. Father used to be a clever man, with a strong will
and a capacity for enjoying everything – I can remember
him like that, and now he's nothing – a complete nonentity
because his spirit's crushed. How could it be otherwise?

69

You've let him down consistently for years – and God knows I'm nothing for him to look forward to – but I might have been if it hadn't been for you – you're not happy – you're never happy – you're fighting – fighting all the time to keep your youth and your looks – because you can't bear the thought of living without them – as though they mattered in the end . . . . You're not young or beautiful; I'm seeing for the first time how old you are – it's horrible – your silly fair hair – and your face all plastered and painted – (*As she flings herself down on the bed, going to her.*) Mother! Mother – sit up – Mother – I have a slight confession to make – (*Taking a small gold box from his pocket.*) Look. . . . Why do you look so shocked? . . . What does it matter? . . . It's only just the beginning. It can't possibly matter – now. (*Reacting to her offer to help him.*) . . . How could you possibly help me? Shut up – shut up – don't touch me – Leave go of me . . . (*Breaks away from her and sweeps everything from her dressing table onto the floor.*) Now then! Now then! You're not to have any more lovers; you're not going to be beautiful and successful ever again – you're going to be my mother for once – it's about time I had one to help me, before I go over the edge altogether – Promise me to be different – you've got to promise me! . . . I love you, really – that's why it's so awful.

It's Ralph
Hugh Whitemore

Dave is a young builder-decorator-plumber. He has long hair and a beard and looks remarkably like Jesus Christ. He wears robe-like white overalls. Ironically his first entrance coincides with another character recalling that his mother always told him to behave himself and . . . 'be a good little boy because Jesus might come knocking at the front door any moment just to check up on me' . . . The scene is a timbered farmhouse converted into a weekend retreat. Andrew, a writer and his wife Clare are there for the weekend when Ralph, a friend from Andrew's past arrives. Andrew, who doesn't remember him, becomes increasingly angered by Ralph's bizarre and dramatic memories. He gets rid of him on a pretext, but Ralph returns, and is then killed when the ceiling collapses on him. Dave's speech ends the play.

Time: The present.

DAVE. Poor old Ralph. I'd never seen anyone dead before. (*Pause.*) Actually that's not true. There was someone. My Dad's auntie. She was funny in the head. She thought she could flap her arms up and down and fly like a bird. They had her put away. But then, when she got older, Dad thought she should come and live with us. We had a house in the country, in Essex. Dad thought she should end her days with the family and not in a loony bin. The house was very unusual. Tall and thin. And there was trees all round it. There was a gap in the trees, and through that gap you could see the Colchester to London railway line. My old aunt loved to watch the trains go by. They gave her a room on the top floor so she could see the trains clearly. They kept the window locked, just in case. One day she managed to prise the window open. She crawled onto the window-sill, flapped her arms up and down, and jumped. Poor old darling. Mum rushed out and found her. 'Don't look,' she said, but of course I did. Wasn't nasty or frightening. Just a funny bundle of clothes with legs and arms sticking out of it. Mum said it was a blessed release. She often said that about people dying. (*Pause.*) I suppose some people thought she killed herself because we kept her locked up and were cruel to her. Perhaps some people thought she was trying to escape and killed herself accidentally. Some people knew the truth, of course. And perhaps there was someone in a train going from Colchester to London. And perhaps he looked out of the window, and perhaps, through the gap in the trees, he saw an old lady in mid-air, flapping her arms up and down. Just for a split-second, as the train rushed on, past our house. And he'd look through the window, that man, and he'd be amazed. He'd tell his friend, 'I saw an old lady flying', he'd say. So in a way, it actually happened. What she wanted. Perhaps she died happy. What do you think?

The Roses of Eyam
Don Taylor

The Great Plague started in the village of Eyam, Derbyshire and the play is set there. Each day more villagers die, and here the local madman, known as the Bedlam, watches and talks of the sad happenings in his own strange way.
Time: 1665.
Note: Two short speeches have been joined here.

BEDLAM. I seen it, I seen it! (*Whispers as though a secret.*) Three new graves, open in the churchyard. I laughed and danced, but they sent me away. They don't think it's funny, putting a man in a hole. . . . (*Sees a procession with a coffin.*) . . . They've got Peter Halksworth in that long box. . . . They've nailed him in. In case he changes his mind. . . . (*A second cortège appears.*) . . . They've put Thomas Thorpe in that one, because he didn't wake up this morning when they shook him. And in that one his wife Mary. Just because her toes went black. They owned a shop. But last night a white cricket sang at the back door, and this morning the shutters are closed. . . . They've stopped all the music, and planted them in the earth. Perhaps they think they'll grow, like flowers. . . . (MOMPESSON *enters.*) . . . Mister! . . . Can I come with you? . . . I been playing in the grass by the church! I seen four graves. Four. . . . There's one all grass. Not opened yet. . . . (MOMPESSON *leaves and* BEDLAM *shouts after him, his words gradually becoming terrified.*) . . . And I seen another one, and another, and another, all in a line, and black buds on all the trees, and a forest of crosses growing up in the street, and over the river and all across the valley, till it's all thick and dark, no more people, just big black trees . . . ! (*Alone*.) . . . Nobody listens to the mad boy. . . .

He turns in circles, holding up his hands as though catching snowflakes.

Snow – snow – snow – I'm going to build a snowman for Christmas. I'll make him big and strong like Marshall Howe, with a hat and a clay pipe, and a stick in his hand. He'll be all right while it stays freezing. But when it gets warmer his face will go black and dirty, and he'll get old, and when the sun comes out again, I'll watch him melt away to a little pool of dirty water. Then he'll be all gone, and there'll be nothing left except his hat and his clay pipe and his stick, and I expect I'll wonder why I bothered to make him at all. . . . (*He looks very sad for a second, then bends down scrabbling in the snow and making noises.*) Nobody listens to the mad boy! (*Exits, bell tinkling.*)

The Gut Girls
Sarah Daniels

The play is set mainly in the gutting shed of the slaughterhouse at the cattle market in Deptford at the turn of the century. Annie, aged 16, is the 'new girl'. She worked previously as a servant, and since the stillbirth of her illegitimate baby, lives in a home for 'friendless girls'. She is at first shocked and sickened by the foul conditions in the meat gutting sheds. In this scene she has made friends with an older girl, Ellen, and is visiting her room.

ANNIE. I was in service, oh, not round here, no, in a beautiful house in Blackheath, and I was real proud of meself, oh, I was. The master and mistress was all right, never thrashed you or anything, they was above that. Had a son at Oxford University, really nice spoken, educated gentleman. When he came home in the holiday, he wouldn't let me be. In front of anybody, I mean, he treated me like dirt, but would creep up on me when no one was about. I fought him. I pleaded with him, I threatened him, but he'd laugh. His mama would never believe it of her darling son. Oh, and I wasn't the only one, and it didn't only happen once and when I fell, that was it – got shot of me. I 'ad nowhere ter go, nowhere. I walked the streets and I was picked up and taken to be examined – six months gone I was – for diseases, to them I was a prostitute and the way they treat you and the way they look at you, and the way they hate you, and the way they blame you and everyone blames me. But I never cried, not one of them saw me cry and when I got to that home, it was awful but it was heaven. And even when I was told it was dead I never cried. Why don't they tell

75

you birth is such an awful, bloody, terrible, painful thing. It was born with the cord round its neck. It had strangled itself the poor, poor, little tiny thing and I looked at it before they took it away (*Bitterly.*) and I thought, you lucky, lucky bastard, how much better if I'd have been born like that.

She starts to sob for the first time since the baby was born. ELLEN looks at her and puts her arms round her and lets her cry.

Note: *The Gut Girls* was first performed at the Albany Empire, London on 2 November 1988.

Hindle Wakes
Stanley Houghton

The scene is the breakfast room of the Jeffcote's house in Hindle
Vale at 9 p.m. on Tuesday August 7, 1912. Fanny Hawthorn,
a weaver at Daisy Bank Mill in Hindle, Lancs, has spent the
weekend with Alan Jeffcote, son of the mill owner. Although
Alan is engaged to Beatrice Farrar, a girl of his own class,
the respective fathers decide that he and Fanny must wed.
But Fanny, a young girl with a mind of her own, has not
been reckoned with. Fanny is about 17, sturdy, determined
and attractive.

FANNY. Don't you kid yourself, my lad! It isn't because
I'm afraid of spoiling YOUR life that I'm refusing you, but
because I'm afraid of spoiling MINE! . . . I don't know
as money's much to go by when it comes to a job of this
sort. It's more important to get the right chap. Suppose
it didn't last? Weddings brought about this road have a
knack of turning out badly. Would you ever forget it was
your father bade you marry me? No fear! You'd bear me a
grudge all my life for that. You wouldn't be able to help it.
You're a nice, clean, well-made lad. Oh, ay! I like you right
enough. . . . I WAS fond of you, in a way. . . . But love
you? Good heavens, of course not! Why on earth should I
love you? You were just someone to have a bit of fun with.
You were an amusement – a lark. . . . How much more did
you care for me? You're a man and I was your little fancy.
Well, I'm a woman and YOU were MY little fancy. You
wouldn't prevent a woman enjoying herself as well as a man,
if she takes it into her head? . . . You're not good enough
for me. The chap Fanny Hawthorn weds has got to be made

of different stuff from you, my lad. MY husband, if I ever have one, will be a man, not a fellow who'll throw over his girl at his father's bidding! Strikes me the sons of these rich manufacturers are all much alike. They seem a bit weak in the upper storey. It's their father's brass that's too much for them, happen! They don't know how to spend it properly. They're like chaps who can't carry their drink because they aren't used to it. The brass gets into their heads like! . . . You're not a fool altogether. But there's summat lacking. You're not man enough for me. . . . We've had a right good time together, I'll never forget that. But all good times have to come to an end and ours is over now. Come along now, and bid me farewell. . . . (*Holding out her hand.*) Goodbye, old lad.

Same Old Moon
Geraldine Aron

*Bella Rafferty, aged 17, is described as the town tart, able to
dance, big, brazen, and full of herself. She has called on her
neighbours in order to use the mirror of their wardrobe. In this
scene she is talking to 11-year-old Brenda, who lives there in
Galway with her Granny Cleary and strange Aunty Peace, who
is about to leave the room in disgust at Bella's conversation.*
Time: 1951.

BELLA. Stay with me, Brenda, and learn about the
interesting side of life. (AUNTY PEACE *goes*.) God, your
Aunty Peace is awful crabby, Brenda. But I suppose she
never really recovered from that bullseye business. . . . Do
you mean to tell me you don't know what caused your Aunty
Peace's bad nerves and poor eyesight? Well, you must be the
only person in Galway that *doesn't* know. Two boys from St
Luke's Reformatory followed her to the tidal pool one day.
'Tell me,' says one of them, 'are you fond of bull's eyes?'
'Course I am,' says your Aunty Peace, 'bullseyes are my
favourites.' 'Well we put a couple in your blazer pockets for
you,' says the other lad, 'we thought you'd be hungry after
your swim.' 'Thanks very much,' says your Aunty Peace.
And didn't she put her hands into her blazer pockets and
didn't she draw out two big bull's eyes, a right and a left,
fresh from the butchers, with bits of veins and *schkin* and
eyelashes still attached to them.

C'mere young one. C'mere till I tell you a secret – and I'll
break your face if you say a word about it. I was in Café
Daphne's yesterday and didn't this fella with a moustache
invite me over to his table! 'Have a cup of tea and a few

79

cakes', says he, pushing the plate over. I accepted the tea but I wouldn't give him the satisfaction of having a cake. A cup of tea is nothing, but a fella like that might think I'd be gawping over a few ould cakes. Anyway: 'You've lovely eyes,' says he, 'are you a visitor from Dublin?'. I told him I wasn't, sipping the tea as if I couldn't be bothered. 'You're never a local girl,' says he, 'you've the air of a big place like Dublin on you.' 'And what air is on you?' says I . . . He said he was on holidays – *from the Seminary*! And I said he better not be admiring my eyes so, and he a priest. 'I'm not a priest *yet*,' says he, 'will you go for a walk?' 'Oh,' says I, 'I thought you'd be in a car with all the smart talk.' 'I've a car parked outside,' says he. 'I'm not sure I could be bothered,' says I, and asked him had it a hood on it. It had. A big black thing – the likes of what you'd see on a baby's pram. Next thing the two of us are on a spin out the coast road. 'Tell me now,' says I, 'when you've your dog collar on, does it stick in your Adam's apple?' He said it did and asked me would I kiss the place better. I did – and he kissed the beauty spot behind my ear, so I told him to stop the car quick for fear of an accident! The compliments he had for me! He said they'd told him at the Seminary he must expose himself to the world outside before making his final decision – that's why he was on holidays, testing himself to see could he resist temptation. (*Giving a cheeky laugh.*) His Guardian Angel will be wore out so, because his nibs and I have another date this evening. That's where I'm going now and I twenty minutes late on purpose! . . . And when it's all over I'm going to open my big eyes and look at him and say, 'Could you ever bless me, Father?' Can you imagine the face he'll have on him? I'll tell you something: I could get anyone to love me! *Anyone* – even the Pope! (*She laughs and poses, in love with herself.*)

Vanity Fair
William Makepeace Thackeray

*Becky Sharp and her much richer, more ladylike friend, Amelia
Sedley, are leaving Miss Pinkerton's Academy for Young Ladies.
Amelia, loved and popular will be sadly missed. Becky has
always been troublesome . . . her father, once the Academy's
drawing master, died drunk and penniless, leaving a letter begging
Miss Pinkerton to educate his daughter. As her mother had some
education and Becky spoke French she was taken on sufferance as
an 'articled pupil' to speak French with the pupils and to live cost
free. She has been there two years, and is on her way to spend a
short time with Amelia's family before taking up a post. Becky at
19 is described as small, slight, pale, attractive, sharp, witty and
precocious. . . . The girls are in the carriage having been presented
with their leaving gifts of 'Dixionaries'.*

Time: 1815.

BECKY. So much for the Dixionary; and thank God I'm
out of Chiswick. . . . Why, what's the matter, Amelia? Do
you think Miss Pinkerton will come out and order me back
to the black hole? . . . I hate the whole house. I hope I may
never set eyes on it again. I wish it were in the bottom of the
Thames, I do; and if Miss Pinkerton were there, I wouldn't
pick her out, that I wouldn't. O how I should like to see
her floating in the water yonder, turban and all, with her
train streaming after her, and her nose like the beak of a
wherry. . . . Hush, indeed, Amelia! Why, hush? Will the
black footman tell tales? He may go back and tell Miss
Pinkerton that I hate her with all my soul, and I wish he
would; and I wish I had a means of proving it, too. For two
years I have only had insults and outrage from her. I have
been treated worse than any servant in the kitchen. I have

81

never had a friend, or a kind word, except from you. I have
been made to tend the little girls in the lower schoolroom,
and to talk French to the Misses, until I grew sick of my
mother-tongue. But that talking French to Miss Pinkerton
was capital fun, wasn't it? She doesn't know a word of
French, and was too proud to confess it. I believe it was
that which made her part with me; and so thank heaven for
French. Vive la France! Vive l'Empereur! Vive Bonaparte!
. . . It is of no matter to me, Amelia, whether you think I
should not dare to have such wicked, revengeful thoughts!
. . . Revenge may be wicked, but it's natural . . . and I'm
no angel. I am most certainly not!

The Black Prince
Iris Murdoch

Julian Baffin is a 20-year-old student, in love with a much older friend of her parents, Bradley Pearson. Bradley, a failed writer, has been helping Julian with her study of Hamlet. Earlier in the play she has described to him her playing of Hamlet in a school production, wearing black tights, black velvet shoes with silver buckles, a sort of black slinky jerkin with a low neck, a white silk shirt and a big gold chain.

The scene is in Bradley's sitting room.

Time: the present.

JULIAN. How old are you Bradley? . . . (*Slightly shaken at his reply.*) Oh – forty-two – well, I don't call that old. Bradley, don't be so horrid to me. (*She reaches out a hand.*) . . . To a nunnery go, and quickly too – It doesn't occur to you that I might return your love? . . . (*In reply to his 'No'.*) I've known you all my life, I've always loved you. I was so happy when you came to see my father and I could ask you things and tell you things – so many things weren't real at all until I'd told you them – you were a sort of touchstone of reality to me. If you only knew how much I've always admired you. When I was a little child I used to say I wanted to marry you. Do you remember? All right, you don't! You've been my ideal man for ever and ever. This isn't just a silly child's thing, it's real deep love, of course it's a love I haven't questioned or thought about or even named until quite lately – but now I have questioned it and thought about it – now that I'm grown up. You see, my love has grown up too. I've so much wanted to be with you and know you properly – since I've been a woman.

Why do you think I wanted to discuss *Hamlet?* I did want to discuss *Hamlet*, but I much more wanted your affection, your attention, I wanted to *look* at you. I've *longed* to touch you and kiss you in these last years, oh years, only I didn't dare to, I never thought I would. I've been thinking about you all the time – I love you, I love you.

The Arcata Promise
David Mercer

When Laura is 16 she is left by her American parents at school in England, and meets John, an actor in his early thirties. Later, against parental wishes, she lives with him in London. Success, under his assumed name of Theodore Gunge, and excessive drinking, lead to rows, problems and the disintegration of their relationship. The play's title refers to the love pact made in Arcata, USA, which Laura, now aged 20, breaks in her decision to leave Gunge. Originally a TV play in 1974. The scene takes place in Gunge's Chelsea flat.

LAURA. I came to live with you because I loved you. I stayed with you because I loved you. (*Pause.*) I endured you because I couldn't imagine life without you. (*Pause.*) I feel *battered*. Ignored. Belittled. (*Pause.*) I didn't care for you because you're a famous actor. You remember talking about that party where we met? Well when *you* came over and talked to *me* – I thought I'd never seen a man so haunted. So defensive and uptight. (*Pause.*) I never thought you'd find me attractive. I never thought you'd see me again. (*Pause.*) When you asked me to, I said yes for *you*. Not because I was impressed, or flattered, or anything like that. I almost didn't *dare* to think you'd have any serious interest in me. (*Pause.*) But you did. (*Pause.*) Girls at school used to laugh at me because I said I wouldn't go to bed until it was somebody I loved. *Very* old-fashioned, or whatever. At my school you were considered freaky if you were still a virgin after sixteen. (*Pause.*) And because of you – I was *glad*. I was happy I'd never been with anyone else. (*Pause.*) I've been happy with you – but too sad as well. Too humiliated.

(*Pause.*) Too hurt. (*Pause.*) I never thought it mattered at all your being so much older. Now I can see it does. Not the years. Not the difference in experience. (*Pause.*) It's that you'll go on being exactly the same. (*Her voice rising.*) And I'm *changing*. . . . (*Standing.*) I've loved you. I believe you love me. But you've lived and behaved exactly as you wanted – with me like some kind of appendage. (*Pause.*) Where have I been? Who did anybody ever think I was? Some of your friends still can't even remember my surname! Others pity me. I can count on one hand the number of times I've ever been asked a question about myself. I imagine people find me dull and boring. You drink. You talk. You dominate. *I'm* the one who drives you home. You rant. You rave. You're the evening's entertainment. I'm the one you turn on when we get home. I should think I'm despised. Not because anyone's taken the trouble to find out what I'm like. No. But because I must seem like your bloody shadow. (*Pause.*) I'm not envious. I admire your acting and respect it as much as anybody else does. But I'm not just a servicing arrangement to your needs. I'm *something* else. (*Pause.*) And I'm going to find out what that is.

Shakers
John Godber and Jane Thornton

The four characters in Shakers *are long-suffering waitresses in the town's trendy cocktail bar. During the play the girls switch from role to role giving the audience insight into the many types the bar attracts. But each girl is given a chance to reveal something of her life outside Shakers. Nicki, aged about 20, has always wanted to act; in her speech she tells the others about her chosen audition piece.*

Place: Shakers Cocktail Bar, in any major city.

Time: The 1980s.

NICKI. It is something that I've put together myself. Er . . . I've written all the words down on a bit of paper so you can test me. Yeah. Right. It's called *The Smile.* (*Pause.*) Right I'll start shall I? (*Pause.*) I'm a bit nervous, so it might be a bit shit. She'd been in hospital for about four days. She was seventy. She went into hospital for an hysterectomy; the operation had been a great success. I went to see her and she looked great, she even showed me the stitches. She's my gran, by the way. So at work, I was having a laugh and a good time. Then they rang, the hospital, said she'd had a stroke. So I went on the bus to the hospital, I felt sick, travelling all that way on a bus. She was on the sixth floor, I remember that, in a side cubicle in a ward full of old ladies. I walked into the room. My mam and dad were looking out of the window, looking across the parkland of the hospital. And my uncle and auntie were there, looking out of the window; they were crying. My gran was laid in bed; half of her face was blue and deformed, her mouth was all twisted and taut, one eye was closed. She looked at me, and tried to smile. I remember the crying in the background. She tried to speak, but said nothing. She just laid there. 'Hello gran,' I said. 'Hello. What's all this bloody nonsense about having a stroke? Eh?' And she just smiled at me. She just smiled.

Adam Bede
George Eliot

Hetty, a young country girl is to hang for the crime of killing
her unwanted, illegitimate baby. Dinah, a loving, mature and
compassionate young woman, who is also a Methodist preacher,
is trying to give her strength in her last hours. Dinah is very
attractive, her beauty not disguised despite the sombre Quaker-like
cap and dress she wears. George Eliot based the character on her
own Methodist Aunt Samuel.
    Setting: a cell in Stoniton Jail.
    Time: 1800.

DINAH. Hetty . . . do you know who it is that sits by your
side? . . . Yes, it's Dinah. . . . And do you remember the
time when we were at the Hall Farm together, and that
night when I told you to be sure and think of me as a
friend in trouble. . . . Hetty, I can't save you from death
on Monday. But isn't the suffering less hard when you have
somebody with you, that feels for you – that you can speak
to, and say what's in your heart? . . . Yes, Hetty: you lean
on me: you are glad to have me with you. . . . I won't leave
you. I'll stay with you to the last. . . . But, Hetty, there
is someone else in this cell besides me, someone close to
you. . . . Someone who has been with you through all your
hours of sin and trouble – who has known every thought
you have had – has seen where you went, where you lay
down and rose up again, and all the deeds you have tried
to hide in darkness. And on Monday, when I can't follow
you – when my arms can't reach you – when death has
parted us, – he who is with us now, and knows all, will be
with you then. It makes no difference – whether we live or

89

die, we are in the presence of God. My poor Hetty, death is very dreadful to you. I know it's dreadful. But if you had a friend to take care of you after death – in that other world – someone whose love is greater than mine – who can do everything? . . . If God our Father was your friend, and was willing to save you from sin and suffering, so as you should neither know wicked feelings nor pain again? If you could believe he loved you and would help you, as you believe I love you, and will help you, it wouldn't be so hard to die on Monday, would it? Hetty, you are shutting up your soul against him, by trying to hide the truth. God's love and mercy can overcome all things – our ignorance, and weakness, and all the burthen of our past wickedness – all things but our wilful sin; sin that we cling to, and will not give up. You believe in my love and pity for you, Hetty; but, if you had not let me come near you, if you wouldn't have looked at me or spoken to me, you'd have shut me out from helping you: I couldn't have made you feel my love; I couldn't have told you what I felt for you. Don't shut God's love out in that way, by clinging to sin. . . . It is sin that brings dread, and darkness, and despair: there is light and blessedness for us as soon as we cast it off: Cast it off now, Hetty – now: confess the wickedness you have done – the sin you have been guilty of against your heavenly Father. Let us kneel down together, for we are in the presence of God. Hetty, we are before God: he is waiting for you to tell the truth.

Plenty
David Hare

As a young girl during the Second World War, Susan Traherne served with British Intelligence as a courier in occupied France. In 1947 when this scene takes place, Susan, now 21, has been holidaying in Belgium with Tony Radley, a colleague from the war years. He has died very suddenly, and Susan, travelling as Mrs Radley, goes to the Embassy where she is interviewed by a diplomat, Raymond Brock. The effects of the war on Susan, the disillusionment she feels about post-war Britain are beginning to be visible, but as yet there are no signs of her mental illness.

SUSAN. Tony was a wireless operator with SOE. Our job was harassment behind the lines. Very successful in Holland. Denmark. Less so in France. Tony was in a circuit the Gestapo destroyed. Then scattered. Ravensbruch, Buchenwald, Saarbrucken, Dachau. Some were tortured, executed. . . . I was a courier. I was never caught. (*She looks straight at* BROCK.) I wasn't his wife . . . . Motoring together it was easier to say we were man and wife. In fact I was barely even his mistress. He simply rang me a few weeks ago and asked if I'd like a holiday abroad. I was amazed. People in our organisation really didn't know each other all that well. You made it your business to know as little as possible, it was a point of principle. Even now you don't know who most of your colleagues were. Perhaps you were in it. Perhaps I met you. I don't know. (*Pause.*) . . . Tony I knew a bit better, not much, but I was glad when he rang. Those of us who went through this kind of war, I think we do have something in common. It's a kind of impatience, we're rather intolerant, we don't suffer fools.

91

And so we get rather restless back in England, the people who stayed behind seem childish and a little silly. I think that's why Tony needed to get away. If you haven't suffered . . . well. And so driving through Europe with Tony I knew that at least I'd be able to act as I pleased for a while. That's all. (*Pause.*) It's kind of you not to have told the ambassador. . . . He had a wife. And three children. I had to lie about those, I couldn't claim them somehow. She lives in Crediton, in Devon. She believes that Tony was travelling alone. He'd told her he needed two weeks by himself. That's what I was hoping you could do for me. 'Phone her. I've written the number down. I'm afraid I did it before I came. . . . I'd prefer it if you lied. But it's up to you. (*She looks at* BROCK. *Pause.*) It was an innocent relationship. That doesn't mean unphysical. Unphysical isn't innocent. Unphysical in my view is repressed. It just means there was no guilt. I wasn't particularly fond of Tony, he was very slow-moving and egg-stained if you know what I mean, but we'd known some sorrow together and I came with him. And so it seemed a shocking injustice when he fell in the lobby, unjust for him of course, but also unjust for me, alone, a long way from home, and worst of all for his wife, bitterly unfair if she had to have the news from me. Unfair for life. And so I approached the Embassy.

The Old Bachelor
William Congreve

*A play with the themes of deceit and disguise, popular at the
time, 1693. Belinda and her cousin, Araminta, both have money.
Araminta, to whom Belinda is talking here, is the more serious and
sincere. Belinda is described as 'excessively foppish, and affected,
and a baggage' by one character, and 'too proud, too inconstant,
too affected, too witty and too handsome for a wife'.*
Scene: St James's Park, London.

BELINDA. Lard, my dear! I am glad I have met you.
I have been at the Exchange[1] since, and am so tired –
Oh, the most inhuman, barbarous hackney-coach! I am
jolted to a jelly. – Am I not horridly touzed?[2] (*Pulls out
a pocket-glass.*) O frightful! What a furious fiz I have! O
most rueful! Ha, ha, ha! O gad. I hope nobody will come
this way till I put myself a little in repair. – Ah, my dear
– I have seen such unhewn creatures since, ha, ha, ha! I
can't for my soul help thinking that I look just like one of
'em. Good dear, pin this, and I'll tell you. – Very well. –
So, thank you, my dear. – But as I was telling you – pish,
this is the untoward'st lock. – So, as I was telling you –
how d'ye like me now? Hideous, ha? Frightful still? Oh
how? And so – but where did I leave off, my dear? I
was telling you – Oh, a most comical sight! A country
squire, with the equipage of a wife and two daughters,
came to Mrs Snipwel's shop while I was there. – But, oh
gad, two such unlicked cubs! Ay, o' my conscience; fat as
a barn-door fowl, but so bedecked you would have taken 'em
for Friezland-hens, with their feathers growing the wrong
way. – O such outlandish creatures! Such Tramontanae,[3]

93

and foreigners to the fashion, or anything in practice! I had not patience to behold. – I undertook the modelling of one of their fronts, the more modern structure. The poor creature, I warrant, was as full of courtesies as if I had been her godmother. The truth on't is, I did endeavour to make her look like a Christian – and she was sensible of it, for she thanked me, and gave me two apples, piping hot, out of her under-petticoat pocket, ha, ha, ha. And t'other did so stare and gape – I fancied her like the front of her father's hall; her eyes were the two jut-windows, and her mouth the great door, most hospitably kept open for the entertainment of travelling flies. Why, the father bought a powder-horn, and an almanac, and a comb-case; the mother, a great fruz-tour,[4] and a fat amber necklace; the daughters only tore two pair of kid gloves with trying 'em on – Oh gad, here comes the fool that dined at my Lady Freelove's t'other day. (*Enter* SIR JOSEPH *and* BLUFFE.) We'll put on our masks to secure his ignorance.

1 *Exchange*: shops on the south side of the Strand.
2 *touzed*: dishevelled.
3 *Tramontanae*: dwelling or situated beyond the mountains; here: uncouth, unpolished.
4 *fruz-tour*: high, curled frontlet of false hair.

Keeping Tom Nice
Lucy Gannon

This play is about looking after Tom, a man of 24, severely physically disabled, unable to communicate, to feed or tend himself, to walk or pick up anything for himself. It is not known how intelligent Tom is, but we do know he uses language internally. Charlie is Tom's 23-year-old sister, a mature student at University. She is described as bright, apparently loving, but immature. She is desperate to help Tom to feel emotion, to grow and to move out of the terrible dull predictability of his static existence.

Time: The present.

CHARLIE. Right, Tom. Time for an update. Update time. Star date . . . Where did we get to? I told you about the river . . . and the bridges . . . now, let's see. People. Where will I start? Well, there's Sheila. She's, oh, I dunno, about thirty-five, forty . . . old anyway. She wears black overalls from Millets and she drinks real ale and cries into it because none of the men fancy her! Then she gets pissed and she sits in the corner glaring at the men and muttering 'castrate the bastards!' and 'Ireland for the Irish' and all that sort of stuff. Anyway, she's sex mad. Permanently randy. Bernadette says she had a transplant and they made a terrible mistake and gave her fully functioning monkey glands. You'd like Bernadette. She's only there at weekends. She's a Catholic. She works in a steakhouse and she's in love with this horrible old married man. Manager of a cut price supermarket. Really gross. To add insult to injury she turned vegan last week. Can you believe it, Tom? A sinning Catholic vegan serving up bloody steaks all day long. My God, it's pure Edna O'Brien! And the town! Oh, God, I wish

I could show you the town, Tommy. I walk around it, saying to myself, 'You're here, Charlie. Here. Look. Look and remember.' I don't want to forget any of it, not one bit of it! And the gigs! Oh, no, I was telling you about the town. Remind me about the bands, eh? This is me, going out to a lecture. Slam the door, scramble past the bikes in the passage, bloody things. Down the steps, one, two, three. There! And the street's so narrow – a back street in any other town, and God! There's loads of us, some in a rush, some strolling, great gangs all talking together, no one looking where they're going, like some big noisy crab, sideways. Some riding bikes. Millions riding bikes! Here comes one now – looking back over his shoulder calling to someone – he hasn't seen me, damn man! (*She flattens herself against an imaginary wall and flops down with relief at his passing.*) Phew! He's gone! (*She laughs and caresses* TOM's *face, then grows suddenly quiet, reflective.*) And it's all so lonely. I sit in my room and I think of you, Tom. I think of you and wonder about you. It's nothing like I'd imagined. And I can't tell Dad, can I? You're doing it for all of us, Charlotte, consolation for how things are. Consolation prize. Oh, Tom. Twenty-four-years-old and stuck here with Mum and Dad. You're looking at me, Tom and I haven't a bloody clue what you're making of all this. If you're making anything of it at all. Are you with me, Tom? Are you? Talcumed and combed and laid to rest on a clean and comfy bean bag . . . (*He laughs apparently involuntarily as a baby laughs with wind, and this suddenly angers her.*) Do you give a damn what happens to me? Do you? Wasting my time. Wasting my time, because you don't care, do you? You don't give a damn if I'm here or there or dead or bloody gone, do you? I'm sorry, Tom. I'm sorry. You do care, don't you? You do listen. It's our bargain, isn't it? If I talk, you'll listen.

A Woman Killed With Kindness
Thomas Heywood

*Anne Frankford, wife of a good and loving husband, succumbs
to the persistent advances of his so-called friend, Wendoll. When
Frankford discovers her adultery he decides that her punishment
shall be to be treated with kindness, and sent to live comfortably
in another of his houses, never to see or contact him, or their two
children again. The play, an Elizabethan domestic tragedy, was
written in 1603.*

ANNE (*to* NICHOLAS). If you return unto your master say –
    Though not from me, for I am all unworthy
    To blast his name with a strumpet's tongue –
    That you have seen me weep, wish myself dead.
    Nay, you may say too, for my vow is pass'd,
    Last night you saw me eat and drink my last.
    This to your master you may say and swear,
    For it is writ in Heaven and decreed here.

    . . .

    Go break this lute upon my coach's wheel,
    As the last music that I e'er shall make,
    Not as my husband's gift but my farewell
    To all earth's joy; and so your master tell.

    . . .

    You have beheld the wocfullest wretch on earth,
    A woman made of tears. Would you had words
    To express but what you see. My inward grief
    No tongue can utter, yet unto your power
    You may describe my sorrow, and disclose
    To thy sad master my abundant woes.

You'll do my commendations? Oh no,
I dare not so presume; nor to my children.
I am disclaim'd in both; alas, I am.
Oh, never teach them when they come to speak
To name the name of mother; chide their tongue
If they by chance light on that hated word;
Tell them tis naught. For when that word they name,
Poor pretty souls, they harp on their own shame.
I have no more to say. Speak not for me;
Yet you may tell your master what you see.

. . .

Exit NICHOLAS.

So, now unto my coach, then to my home
So to my deathbed, for from this sad hour
I never will nor eat, nor drink, nor taste
Of any cates[1] that may preserve my life.
I never will nor smile, nor sleep, nor rest;
But when my tears have wash'd my black soul white,
Sweet Saviour, to Thy hands I yield my sprite.

WENDOLL *approaches*.

Oh, for God's sake fly!
The devil doth come to tempt me ere I die.
My coach! This fiend that with an angel's face
Courted mine honour till he sought my wrack
In my repentant eyes seems ugly black.

1 *cates*: food.

98

Hush
April De Angelis

*When Jo drowned a year ago she left the house by the sea to her
15-year-old daughter Jo, and sister Louise. Weekends are spent
there repairing the neglect, and Denise is helping as a temporary
cleaner. She is 23, has never settled, is gullible, easily influenced
and follows any current trend. She is also kind, lovable and
sometimes exasperating. This evening she is overdressed, hoping
a man she has met will visit; in the meantime Tony, Louise's
husband is on the receiving end of her reminiscing.*

Time: The present.

A long pause.

DENISE. Once I got really pissed. Really pissed at this
party and then I got really hungry, really hungry, you
know, like you do after drinking and so I devoured a bowl
of peanuts. A whole bowl, to myself.

Pause.

And then I vomited the lot back up. I sort of regurgitated
them. The thing is, the thing is, they came out whole. I
must have just swallowed them down without any sort of
chewing. Later someone remarked that they shot out like
bullets. Ping ping. Ping.

Pause.

I was a bit depressed at the time.

Pause.

The reason I'd been depressed was because I'd been working
at this sandwich making job. I was living with this bloke

99

and we were making sandwiches in his flat. At first I really threw myself into it. I experimented with fillings, I bought a butter dish. We used to drive round delivering sandwiches to local businesses only quite often we never got any orders. We ate quite a lot of sandwiches on those occasions. That dealt quite a blow to my enthusiasm I can tell you. Not to mention the fact that I wasn't getting the correct balance of amino acids in my diet. And that can lead to personality disorders. Like shoplifting or slimming. Then one day we found a cockroach lying upside down in a giant size tub of margarine. It wasn't me that left the lid off. That was when the infestation started. You can never be alone with an infestation. Soon after that he left me. He walked out leaving rent arrears and twenty-seven kilos of cheddar. I lay in bed weeping for days. I don't know if what we had was love but it did provide light relief from all the buttering. That was before I became a Buddhist. I used to watch the cockroaches basking on the walls. They do say in the event of a nuclear holocaust cockroaches will survive to inherit the earth. They used to crawl around in a superior manner as if they knew they could survive intense heat and I couldn't. Cocky bastards. The thing is, I'd never go through that now. Be used like that. Because now I'm different. Transformed by experience.

Pause.

Sometimes I wonder what happens. What happens to people who can't find enthusiasm for things. The way things are.

Pause.

Of course there's always acupuncture.

The Cagebirds
David Campton

A group of birds each having the characteristic of a type of woman is imprisoned in a cage. They have become used to their capture and are now unwilling to return to the outside world. The Wild One, who has only just been captured, thinks quite differently, and tries to stir their feelings, to join her in escape.

THE WILD ONE. All right. Let me try to put myself in your place. How long have you been here? Days? Weeks? Months? Years? Have you always been here? Are you content to sit as time slips by – all the days, weeks, months, years, to come? . . . Doesn't anything matter to you beyond aches and food, scandal and the reflection in your mirror? Isn't there room for anything in your mind but prejudice and fear? . . . You are denied your basic human rights and you don't even care. You are prisoners. Are you content with that? I'm just trying to understand you, that's all. Just trying. Did you ever behave like me? Did you ever beat at the door, shout protest slogans, complain about the injustice of it all? Or shall I, given time, become like you . . . secure in my own little space . . . perhaps working out beautiful, complicated, useless plans for escape? Never! Listen to me! You are going to listen to me! (*Goes up to one of them, the* GOSSIP, *and holds her arm.*) Listen . . . the world stretches farther than the few inches between your ears. . . . There is another world outside. (*As the* GOSSIP *breaks away from her she moves to the* GLOOM.) Listen . . . we are going to escape . . . you, me and all the others! . . . A door is only a door. Enough hands can break it down. . . . (*As the* GLOOM *moves off, she tries the* GAZER.) Listen.

We are a majority. . . . There are seven of us to one of her
. . . she is outnumbered. . . . (*The* GAZER *moves away.*)
Listen to me! All of you! You could be free! All of you!
Must I be caged because you lack willpower? (*She pauses,
looks round, gives a rueful laugh.*) I have no right, have I?
No right to commit such an outrage. I come bursting in
. . . . and within minutes turn your comfortable, satisfied,
non-communicating, slave society upside down . . . No, I
didn't. I only tried. I didn't succeed. I couldn't succeed
because you're not alive. You can't be alive because if you
were . . . you'd be charging at that door with me. This very
minute. All shoulders together. Boom! Thud! Pow! Crash!
. . . But there you sit. I haven't the right to stir the dust. I'm
the Wild One who doesn't belong. Ignore her. You have to
ignore her because if you didn't you'd either have to break
out or break down. . . . I'm sorry. . . . No, I'm not, but
it's an accepted figure of speech. I'm sorry, but if you don't
like me you'll have to do the other thing. I'm sorry, but I'm
the Wild One, and the cage has not been built that can hold
me. . . .

*She takes a long run at the door, hurls and hurls herself at it
and, with the impact, collapses into a heap.*

25+
Male and Female

The Three Sisters
Anton Chekhov

Olga, Masha and Irina have high hopes of their clever, gifted brother Andrey becoming a University professor. Instead he marries unsuitably, has children, and a job as Secretary of the local council. In their eyes, and his own, Andrey is something of a failure. The action takes place in the drawing-room of the family home in a county town in Russia around the turn of the century.

ANDREY. I'm sick of them. Where's Olga?

[OLGA *comes out from behind the screen.*]

You're the person I'm looking for. Give me the key to the cupboard, will you – I've lost mine. You know that little key you've got.

[OLGA *silently gives him the key. . .*]

Pause.

What an enormous fire, though! It's begun to die down now. Damn it, he made me so cross, that man Ferapont. That was a stupid thing I said to him . . . Making him call me sir.

Pause.

Why don't you say something, then, Olya?

Pause.

It's time you stopped all this nonsense. It's time you stopped pouting about like that for no earthly reason. You're here, Masha. Irina's here. All right, then, let's have it out in the open, once and for all. What have you three got against me? What is it? . . . I'll just say what I have to say and then I'll go. Forthwith . . . In the first place you've got something against Natasha, my wife – and this I've been aware of from the very day we got married. Natasha is a fine person – honest, straightforward, and upright – that's my opinion. I love and respect my wife – I respect her, you understand? – and I insist that others respect her, too. I say it again – she's an honest and upright person, and all your little marks of displeasure – forgive me, but you're simply behaving like spoilt children.

Pause.

Secondly, you seem to be angry that I'm not a professor, that I'm not a scientist. But I serve in local government, I am a member of the local Council, and this service I consider just as sacred, just as elevated, as any service I could render to science. I am a member of the local Council and proud of it, if you wish to know . . .

Pause.

Thirdly . . . I have something else to say . . . I mortgaged the house without asking your consent . . . To this I plead guilty, and indeed I ask you to forgive me . . . I was driven to it by my debts . . . thirty-five thousand . . . I don't play cards now – I gave it up long since – but the main thing I can say in my own justification is that you're girls, and you get an annuity, whereas I had no . . . well, no income . . .

Pause.

They're not listening. Natasha is an outstanding woman, someone of great integrity. (*Walks about in silence, then stops.*) When I got married I thought we were going to be happy . . . all going to be happy . . . But my God . . . (*Weeps.*) My dear sisters, my own dear sisters, don't believe me, don't trust me . . . (*He goes.*)

Translated by Michael Frayn

Love for Love
William Congreve

*Valentine, a libertine, now run out of cash and credit, is confined
to his rooms with only his servant, Jeremy, for company. With
the bailiff at his back, Jeremy is horrified to hear that his master
intends to display his 'wit' by turning playwright.*
 Setting: Valentine's chamber, London.
 Time: 1695.

JEREMY. Now heaven of mercy continue the tax upon
paper; you don't mean to write! Hem! – Sir, if you please
to give me a small certificate of three lines – only to certify
those whom it may concern: that the bearer hereof, Jeremy
Fetch by name, has for the space of seven years truly and
faithfully served Valentine Legend Esq.; and that he is
not now turned away for any misdemeanour; but does
voluntarily dismiss his master from any future authority
over him – Sir, it's impossible – I may die with you,
starve with you, or be damned with your works; but to
live even three days, the life of a play, I no more expect
it than to be canonized for a muse after my decease. But
sir, is this the way to recover your father's favour? Why,
Sir Sampson will be irreconcilable. If your younger brother
should come from sea, he'd never look upon you again.
You're undone, sir; you're ruined; you won't have a friend
left in the world if you turn poet. – Ah, pox confound that
Will's Coffee-House,[1] it has ruined more young men than
the Royal Oak lottery. Nothing thrives that belongs to't.
The man of the house would have been an alderman by this
time with half the trade, if he had set up in the City. For
my part, I never sit at the door that I don't get double the

stomach that I do at a horse-race. The air upon Banstead Downs is nothing to it for a whetter;[2] yet I never see it, but the spirit of famine appears to me; sometimes like a decayed porter, worn out with pimping, and carrying *billet doux* and songs; not like other porters for hire, but for the jest's sake; now like a thin chairman, melted down to half his proportion with carrying a poet upon tick to visit some great fortune; and his fare to be paid him like the wages of sin, either at the day of marriage, or the day of death. Sometimes like a bilked[3] bookseller, with a meagre terrified countenance, that looks as if he had written for himself, or were resolved to turn author and bring the rest of his brethren into the same condition. And lastly, in the form of a worn-out punk,[4] with verses, in her hand, which her vanity had preferred to settlements, without a whole tatter to her tail, but as ragged as one of the Muses; or as if she were carrying her linen to the paper mill, to be converted into folio books, of warning to all young maids not to prefer poetry to good sense; or lying in the arms of a needy wit, before the embraces of a wealthy fool. (*Enter* SCANDAL.) Mr Scandal, for heaven's sake, sir, try if you can dissuade him from turning poet.

1 *Will's Coffee-House*: well-known coffee-house in Covent Garden that was frequented by writers.
2 *whetter*: stimulant.
3 *bilked*: cheated.
4 *punk*: prostitute.

Up'n'Under
John Godber

The trainer of the Wheatsheaf Arms amateur rugby side has accepted a bet to play and beat the renowned team of the Cobblers Arms. Never having won a single match, success seems unlikely, but nevertheless the team is in training. Amongst them is Phil Hopley, who earlier in the play describes himself as: 'English teacher. Age 29. Weight 160 pounds. Height 5' 8". Position – Stand-Off. Hobbies: Reading, Scrabble, hunting around antique fairs on a Sunday.
Place: Hull. The night before the game.
Time: The present.

PHIL *enters with a hot-water bottle, wearing a dressing-gown.*

PHIL. It's a very funny thing, when I was playing at Loughborough I never got nervous, I never had a thought about the game but tonight I'm like a bag of nerves . . . I've been to the toilet . . . back here to bed . . . I'm going to the toilet again in a minute . . . I'm sweating, sweat's dripping down my brow, even my palms are wet . . . I'll have to hope that I can, well . . . drift off to sleep.

(*Lights change to a red wash covering the stage.*)

And there I was, playing at Wembley in the Challenge Cup Final, playing for Fulham against the mighty Featherstone . . . There was hundreds and hundreds of bloated red faces looking down on me . . . I was on the wing and hundreds of yards away from the rest of the team. Featherstone looked massive . . . I gazed up and caught flashes of their kneecaps . . . They ran through to score, I glimpsed sight of hairs on the palms of their hands. We were losing . . . We needed a try. There was five minutes to play . . . There was an incident off the ball . . . 'Gerroff me, you fat pig.' I saw a gap, big as an ocean opening up in front of me . . . 'Pass the ball . . . pass the ball!' And then it came out of a blur, the ball . . . God, I was nervous . . . I saw it coming towards me . . . daren't take my eye off it . . . I caught it and I ran . . . But I didn't move . . . I looked up . . . and the whole of Featherstone were coming towards me . . . men, women, children . . . miners, shop assistants, garage-owners . . . all on the field after me . . . so I ran . . . but the faster I ran the slower I went . . . I looked around for someone to pass to . . . but they were all having lunch . . . sat down having lunch in the middle of Wembley Stadium . . . 'Go on, Phil,' they said, 'Go on . . . run mate, run' . . . and I was on the underground, going down the Piccadilly Station, running and they were all running after me . . . Then a policeman stopped me and I tried to explain but he wanted my name and where I lived . . . I hit him . . . and ran . . . It was like running in a dream . . . jumping over buildings and landing at different places . . . but wherever I landed they were still there, coming around the corner . . . I ran up an alleyway . . . I was cornered . . . I looked around at them . . . trapped, so I ran . . . I ran towards them . . . I just closed my eyes and ran . . .

Rope
Patrick Hamilton

*It is 1929 and university students, Brandon and Graillo have
murdered a fellow undergraduate for no reason at all, just for
kicks. Daringly they hold a party in the room where the body
lies concealed in a chest. Rupert Cadell, a sophisticated, slightly
effeminate man of 29, very affected in both speech and carriage is a
guest. Rupert is lame in the right leg, and always uses an exquisite
walking stick. This speech comes at the very end of the play when
Rupert has discovered the murder and heard Brandon's boast of
murdering for adventure, for living dangerously. Based on the true
case of Nathan Leopold and Richard Loeb in America in 1924.*

RUPERT. Yes, I know. There's every truth in what you've
said. This is a very queer, dark and incomprehensible
universe, and I understand it little. I myself have always
tried to apply pure logic to it, and the application of logic
can lead us into strange passes. It has done so in this case.
You have brought up my own words in my face, and a man
should stand by his own words. I shall never trust in logic
again. You have said that I hold life cheap. You're right. I
do. Your own included. (*Rises.*)
[BRANDON. What do you mean?]
(*Suddenly letting himself go – a thing he has not done all the
evening, and which he now does with tremendous force, and
clear, angry articulation.*) What do I mean? What do I mean?
I mean that you have taken and killed – by strangulation – a
very harmless and helpless fellow-creature of twenty years.
I mean that in that chest there – now lie the staring and
futile remains of something that four hours ago lived, and
laughed, and ran, and found it good. Laughed as you could

III

never laugh, and ran as you could never run. I mean that, for your cruel and scheming pleasure, you have committed a sin and a blasphemy against that very life which you yourselves now find so precious. And you have done more than this. You have not only killed him; you have rotted the lives of all those to whom he was dear. And you have brought worse than death to his father – an equally harmless old man who has fought his way quietly through to a peaceful end, and to whom the whole Universe, after this, will now be blackened and distorted beyond the limits of thought. That is what you have done. And in dragging him round here tonight, you have played a lewd and infamous jest upon him – and a bad jest at that. And if you think, as your type of philosopher generally does, that all life is nothing but a bad jest, then you will now have the pleasure of seeing it played upon yourselves. . . . What am I doing? It is not what *I* am doing, Brandon. It is what society is going to do. And what will happen to you at the hands of society I am not in a position to tell you. That's its own business. But I can give you a pretty shrewd guess, I think. (*Coming forward to chest and swinging back the lid.*) You are going to hang, you swine! Hang! – both of you! – *hang!*

Has whistle in hand. Runs hobbling to the window, throws it open, leans out, and sends three piercing whistles into the night.

Son of Man
Dennis Potter

A highly individual interpretation of Christ's life from His temptation in the wilderness to the crucifixion. Here Jesus has been talking, after preaching in a hillside village, with Peter, Andrew, James and John, when they are joined by Judas Iscariot from Jerusalem. He draws their attention to the cross in the background.

JESUS (*looks closely at* JUDAS, *who lowers his eyes. Quietly*). I understand where you are from. I understand what you are saying. But what is written is written. What is foretold is foretold. God does not cheat. The son of man must be a man. He must be all of a man. He must pass water like a man. He must get hungry and feel tired and sick and lonely. He must laugh. He must cry. He cannot be other than a man, or else God has *cheated.* (*Urgently.*) And so my Father in Heaven will abandon me to myself. And if my head aches he will not lift the ache out of it. And if my stomach rumbles he will not clean out my bowels. And if a snake curls into my thoughts, then the fang will be in my mind. If I were to have *no* doubt I would be *other than a man.* (*Pause.*) And God does not cheat. (*Silence. The others want to go. With harsh mockery.*) 'We don't like it here, Master.' Too bad. Too flaming bad, my friends. Just look at that cross. Go on! Look at it! So that we can keep it in our minds. (*He taps angrily at his forehead.*) Keep it in here. Keep the shape stinging behind our eyes. And let one little splinter of that bloodied wood stick and fester in our brains. Right? (*He strides up to the cross and holds the upright beam, clinging to it.*) God won't let me alone. Not now. I am His. He burns inside

113

me. He tears at my chest. He lights up my eyes. He tugs at my clothes. Oh Holy Father, you have hunted me down. You have opened the top of my head. I have heard you. I have seen you. Dear Lord God on High – shall I show a man a chair, or shall I show man the truth of your justice and the path to your Kingdom? (*Feverish now, and impressive. The others kneel, except* JUDAS, *who stares wide-eyed at* JESUS.) *Oh, oh, He burns inside me!* The Lord God is in my head and in my eyes and in my heart and in my mouth. Yes, in my mouth. He has told me what to do, what to say. I am His. I am His. I am His. I am the Chosen One. I am the Way. *I am the Messiah. Yes. Yes!* (*Pause.* JESUS *lowers his arms. Now he is calm and matter-of-fact.*) Go into Jerusalem all of you, one by one. Tell the people about Jesus of Nazareth. Tell them He is the One. The One they have been waiting for. Tell them that in three days I shall enter the Holy City on an ass, so fulfilling the prophecies of our forefathers. Tell them to greet me as they would their King. But it is the Kingdom of God I come to honour. Go now! Do as I say! Go! Go!

They rise and move off, and JESUS *turns back to smack at the cross.*

(*Smiling.*) Ach! You should have stayed a tree. A tree. (*Slight pause.*) And I should have stayed a carpenter. A carpenter. (*Pause. Then he follows the others. The light fades.*)

Arden of Faversham
Anon

Arden's wife, Alice, is deceiving him with her lover, Mosby, and eager to have her husband out of the way for good. She solicits the help of Michael, her husband's servant. Usually loyal, Michael, in love with Mosby's sister Susan and fearing to lose her, is persuaded to betray his master's movements to the murderers, Black Will and Shakebag and their accomplice, Greene. Written in 1592, this Elizabethan domestic drama was based on an authentic murder case, and has, at times, been attributed to Shakespeare.

MICHAEL. Well, gentlemen, I cannot but confess,
   Sith you have urged me so apparently,
   That I have vowed my Master Arden's death,
   And he whose kindly love and liberal hand
   Doth challenge nought but good deserts of me
   I will deliver over to your hands.
   This night come to his house at Aldersgate.
   The doors I'll leave unlock'd against you come.
   No sooner shall ye enter through the latch,
   Over the threshold to the inner court,
   But on your left hand shall you see the stairs
   That leads directly to my master's chamber.
   There take him and dispose him as ye please.
   Now it were good we parted company.
   What I have promised I will perform.

Exeunt BLACK WILL, GREENE *and* SHAKEBAG.

   Thus feeds the lamb securely on the down
   Whilst through the thicket of an arbour brake
   The hunger-bitten wolf o'erpries his haunt

And takes advantage to eat him up.
Ah, harmless Arden, how, how hast thou misdone
That thus thy gentle life is levell'd[1] at?
The many good turns that thou hast done to me
Now must I quittance[2] with betraying thee.
I, that should take the weapon in my hand,
And buckler[3] thee from ill-intending foes,
Do lead thee with a wicked, fraudful smile,
As unsuspected, to the slaughterhouse.
So have I sworn to Mosby and my mistress;
So have I promised to the slaughtermen.
And should I not deal currently[4] with them
Their lawless rage would take revenge on me.
Tush, I will spurne at mercy for this once.
Let pity lodge where feeble women lie;
I am resolved, and Arden needs must die.

Exit MICHAEL.

1 *levell'd*: aimed.
2 *quittance*: requite.
3 *buckler*: shield.
4 *currently*: honestly.

Playing Sinatra
Bernard Kops

A middle-aged brother and sister, Norman and Sandra, live together in the large, dilapidated, South London home of their childhood, surrounded by memorabilia of their idol, Frank Sinatra. Sandra dreams of a life away from her childish, manipulative brother, and has become infatuated with a charming stranger, Philip de Groot, a poseur and con-man, in his thirties. Here he visits for the first time. Norman talks of his work repairing the bindings of antique books, and then asks Philip about his life.

Time: The present.

PHILIP. I am a seeker. (*As* SANDRA *hands him tea.*) Ah, how very kind. I used to be an architect. Not bad. Mainly hack work; the exigencies of modern life. The realities. The compromises one has to make. Then, one day, whilst walking in China – I was walking along the Great Wall actually – I had a kind of mystical experience. It was, if you like, my Road to Damascus. An inner voice boomed, 'Philip de Groot! What are you doing with your life?' What was I doing indeed? From that moment on I was plagued with inner doubt. What is the meaning of me? What is the meaning of existence? Is there a meaning? Should there be a meaning? Qui somme nous? Où allons nous? The book is the person, indeed. But my binding fell away. I was terrified. I almost fell apart. (SANDRA *offers him a biscuit.*) Ginger nuts. How very nice. How did you know these were my favourites? Anyway, I survived that greatest crisis in my life. And I chucked it all in. I dabbled in many things, trying to find my new self. I've travelled extensively in India. Did voluntary work amongst the bereft of Africa.

All the time questioning, surviving. You see me as I am, a seeker. I believe we are the stuff that dreams are made of but we, man, humankind, is in terrible danger. And we are the danger. I have a modest income. A legacy. I am content, yet not complacent. I am still searching for my true vocation. I hope that answers your question.

Albert's Bridge
Tom Stoppard

Originally a radio play, it tells the story of Albert, a painter obsessed by his work on a huge girdered railway bridge. It is 'his' bridge and his pride in his work knows no bounds; it finally means more to him than his parents, wife and child. Later in the play his security in his job is threatened.

ALBERT. I shan't wave.

Cut in bridge and painting.

Dip brush, dip brush
without end, come rain or shine;
A fine way to spend my time.
My life is set out for me,
the future traced in brown,
my past measured in silver;
how absurd, how sublime
(don't look down)
to climb and clamber in a giant frame;
dip brush, dip brush, slick, slide wipe
and again.

Painting stops.

I straddle a sort of overflowing gutter on which bathtub boats push up and down. . . . The banks are littered with various bricks, kiddiblocks with windows; dinky toys move through the gaps, dodged by moving dots that have no colour; under my feet the Triang train thunders across the Meccano, and the minibrick estates straggle up over the hill in neat rows with paintbox gardens. It's the most expensive toytown in the store – the detail is remarkable. But fragile. I tremble for it, half expecting some petulant pampered child to step over the hill and kick the whole thing to bits with her Startrite sandals.

Painting.

Don't look down,
the dots are looking up.
Don't wave, don't fall, tumbling down a
telescope, diminishing to a dot.
In eight years who will I be?
Not me.
I'll be assimilated then,
the honest working man, father of three –
you've seen him around,
content in his obscurity, come to terms with public
    truths,
digging the garden of a council house
in what is now my Sunday suit.
I'm okay for fifty years, with any luck;
I can see me climb
up a silver bridge to paint it for the seventh time,
keeping track of my life spent in painting in the
colour of my track:
above it all.
How sublime
(dip brush, dip brush) silvering the brown.
Which dot is mine?
Don't wave, don't look down.
Don't fall.

Breaking the Code
Hugh Whitemore

*Alan Turing, a brilliant mathematician, is renowned for his work
in breaking the famous Enigma Code in the Second World War.
With such top-secret work, his homosexual lifestyle has been cause
for concern in high places. In this scene Alan, now in his early
40's is in Greece, talking to a young man, a holiday lover, who
understands no English. Alan Turing speaks with a stammer.*
    Time: 1953.
    Note: This play is based on the book Alan Turing, The Enigma
by Andrew Hodges.

NIKOS *kisses* TURING, *who is both touched and embarrassed.*

TURING. Thank you, Nikos dear. Thank you. (*He smiles.*)
It's a good feeling, isn't it? Solving a problem, finding the
answer. Making it work. A good feeling. It's all like that
wireless, really; it's all a question of making the right
connections. (*Brief pause; an idea slips into his mind.*) Shall
I tell you a secret? Top secret. I couldn't tell my analyst
about this. But since you won't understand a single word,
it doesn't really matter. It all took place at the beginning of
the war in an English country house called Bletchley Park.
The Germans had built a machine they called the Enigma.
It was very cunning. It made codes – nobody knew how to
break the codes it made. That was the problem we had to
solve. If we didn't, if we couldn't, we'd lose the war – it was
as simple as that. But where to begin? Well, first there was
guesswork. The code-breaking process always began with
a guess. You had to guess what the first few phrases of the
message might mean. This wasn't as difficult as it sounds
because military messages invariably start with a stereotyped
phrase: the date, the time, the name and rank of the sender,

that sort of thing. Then we discovered that it was possible to use the phrase we'd guessed to form a chain of implications, of logical deductions, for each of the rotor positions. If this chain of implications led you to a contradiction – which was usually the case – it meant you were wrong, and you'd have to move on to the next rotor position. And so on and so on and so on. An impossibly lengthy and laborious process. Time was against us; we didn't know what to do. Then, suddenly, one spring afternoon, I remembered a conversation I'd had with Wittgenstein; we were arguing about the fact that a contradiction implies any proposition – and I saw – immediately – that I could use this elementary theorem in mathematical logic to build a machine that would have the necessary speed: a machine with electrical relays and logical circuits which would sense contradictions and recognize consistencies; a machine of cribs, closed loops and perfect synchrony; a machine for discerning a pattern in the patternless. If your guess was wrong, the electricity would flow through all the related hypotheses and knock them out in a flash – like the chain reaction in an atomic bomb. If your hypothesis was correct, everything would be consistent – and the electrical current would stop at the correct combination. Our machine would be able to examine thousands of millions of possibilities at amazing speed, and with any luck, would give us the 'way in'. More than that: all the connections had been made. There was the pure beauty of the logical pattern. The human element. The deeply satisfying relationship between the theoretical and the practical. What a moment that was. Quite, quite extraordinary. (*Pause.*) Oh, Christopher . . . if only you could have been there. Never again. Never again a moment like that. (*Pause.*) In the long run, it's not breaking the code that matters – it's where you go from there. That's the real problem.

The Gift of a Lamb

Charles Causley

A night in winter and three shepherds, grandfather Ben, son John and grandson Dan are out on a hillside. Thieving Jack appears and steals the black and white lamb promised to Dan for his birthday next day. It is also the night of the Nativity. A host of angels and an amazing light appear from on high and Thieving Jack is struck down, then rescued from his plight by the shepherds. Later, at the manger, Dan wants to give Baby Jesus his own birthday lamb and Jack repents.

A version of the old Wakefield Shepherds play.

THIEVING JACK.
(*aside*) Great blocks and bricks,
Now 'ere's a fix –
An' all of me own makin'!
If truth I tell,
To prison-cell
A journey I'll be takin'!
For 'ere I am,
That little lamb
Snug in me thievin' sack . . .

Pause. Then he comes to a decision.

BUT
I'll be strong
An' shame the wrong,
An' dare to give it back.
This Infant King
Of whom they sing
Is merciful and good;

So, from this day,
As best I may,
I'll do things as I should!

He clears his throat loudly and turns towards the SHEP-
HERDS.

Kind shepherds three, who freely gave me aid
When on the 'ill I lay, and was afraid –
Blinded by 'eaven's light, struck by its sound,
Stiff as a stone upon the quakin' ground –
Shepherds, who raised me up and spoke me fair,
Comforted me, an' took me in your care:

A deep breath.

I was no peaceful traveller on the 'ill,
For on your sheepfold I'd long gazed my fill,
And as you watched about your furze-fire bright
I crept, *a robber*, to your flock last night.
The lamb that's black an' white, *I'd* fancied too,
An' thought, 'Why, Jack, that's just the one for you!'
An' so I popped it in the very sack
I bears, so careful-like, upon me back.
See, as I opens it . . .

Faint bleat.

The 'ead appear . . .

Louder bleat.

Its Jacob-coloured coat . . .

Bleat.

The eye, the ear.

Bleat.

And see, my cheek is red,

124

My shame is sore;
I vows I'll go a-thievin' nevermore,
An' give you back the lamb; though well I know
For this night's work to prison I should go.
This price I'll gladly pay; but one thing lack.
Humbly I beg of you – forgive old Jack.

He hands the lamb over to DAN.

Visiting Hour
Richard Harris

*The episodes in this play take place in a hospital. In this one,
subtitled* Going Home, *Cheryl, a white woman, at a crisis point
in her life has grown through her hospital friendship with Tricia,
who is black and a much more whole and successful woman. This
is their last conversation as Tricia is to go home a day early; Cheryl
is in bed, Tricia still in her night-wear with a smart dressing-gown.
They have been discussing 'first impressions' and 'pre-judgements'
of people and Cheryl has tried to explain that she had never really
known a black person before, that she hadn't expected Tricia to be
the sort of person she was. She is groping for words and says 'you
just . . .' and Tricia finishes the sentence for her.*
   Time: The present.

TRICIA. Make assumptions. We all do. I certainly do, I'd
be a liar if I said otherwise. I see Tracy in the bed opposite
scratching her tattoos and moving her mouth as she reads
the *Sun* and, yes I make assumptions. It's whether we're
prepared to break those assumptions down. At least we
owe it to each other to try. (*She smiles, without humour,
and then frowns slightly at the memory.*) Something very –
strange happened the other night . . . the night you were in
the observation ward . . . the entire night staff was black. In
they marched, these five black nurses – including a new girl
I hadn't seen before – and she came round, this new girl, sort
of letting everyone get to know her, and she was trying very
hard, saying how much she liked the flowers, how pretty
someone's hair looked – you know, trying to make all the
right noises . . . and somehow something went wrong. No
one was responding, no one was – reaching out to her –
and the other black nurses were standing back, watching
126

her and smiling . . . and the more anxious she became, the more they smiled, the more satisfied they were, the more they were enjoying it, and one of them came over to me and sat on my bed and said 'you poor baby darling' and stroked my brow and I knew that in that moment – and maybe just in that moment and for no particular reason – those black nurses hated their white patients and those white women were afraid of those black women, they felt threatened by them. Next day (*She shrugs, smiles.*) it was like it never happened. (*Slight pause.*) Most of the women here are like you, they've never come into real contact with a black person and have no way of reading them . . . if they're being funny or ironic or friendly or natural or what . . . and the black person becomes offended because she's trying to communicate, and . . . (*She trails off.*) I see it all the time but I hoped that here, in hospital, the differences would somehow become blurred. But they aren't. Not really. It's just the same.

The Rover
Aphra Behn

It is carnival time and everyone is celebrating in the streets of a Spanish colony. Three well-to-do young women, dissatisfied with their destiny, have disguised themselves as gypsies and are searching for husbands. They have a rival in the famous courtesan, Angellica Bianca, in town on a quest for a rich client. Against her will she falls in love with Willmore. In this scene she holds him at gunpoint and tries to make him admit that he has broken his promise to be faithful to her.

Time: The seventeenth century.

ANGELLICA.
What have you, sir, to say? –
Nay, do not speak

Aside, turning from him

For I know well if I should hear thee out,
Thoud'st talk away all that is brave about me
And I have vowed thy death by all that's sacred.

Follows him with the pistol to his breast.

Nay, Willmore, tell me first . . . tell me how many
Such poor believing fools thou hast undone?
How many hearts thou hast betrayed to ruin?
You said you loved me.
And at that instant I gave you my heart.
I'd price enough and love enough to think
That it could raise thy soul above the vulgar,
Nay, make you all soul too, and soft and constant.
Why did you lie and cheapen me? Alas,

I thought all men were born to be my slaves,
And wore my power like lightning in my eyes;
But when love held the mirror, that cruel glass
Reflected all the weakness of my soul;
My pride was turned to a submissive passion
And so I bowed, which I ne'er did before
To anyone or anything but heaven.
I thought that I had won you and that you
Would value me the higher for my folly.
But now I see you gave me no more than dog lust,
Made me your spaniel bitch; and so I fell
Like a long-worshipped idol at the last
Perceived a fraud, a cheat, a bauble. Why
Didst thou destroy my too long fancied power?
Why didst thou give me oaths? Why didst thou kneel
And make me soft? Why, why didst thou enslave me?

Stage Door

George S Kaufman and Edna Ferber

The play is set in the Footlights Club, a club-hostel for actresses, a brownstone house, large, no longer splendid, in the West Fifties, New York. In this scene, set in one of the bedrooms, Terry returns from the theatre with bad news. Terry Randall is described as having the vivid personality, the mobile face of the born actress, though not conventionally beautiful. She is in her early twenties. Time: The 1930s.

TERRY (*she enters, a drooping figure, closes the door, and slumps against it, looking at her friends*). Young lady, willing, talented, not very beautiful, finds herself at liberty. . . . Will double in brass, will polish brass, will *eat* brass before very long. . . . Hi, girls! . . . We closed. Four performances, and we closed. . . . We just got to the theatre tonight and there it was on the call-board. 'To the Members of the Blue Grotto Company: You are hereby advised that the engagement of the "Blue Grotto" will terminate after tonight's performance. Signed, Milton H. Schwepper, for Berger Productions, Incorporated.' . . . Just like that. We stood there for a minute and read it. Then we sort of got together in the dressing rooms and talked about in whispers, the way you do at a funeral. And then we all put on our make-up and gave the best damned performances we'd ever given. . . . Yes, it was awfully jolly! I wouldn't have minded if Berger or somebody had come backstage and said, 'Look we're sorry to do this to you, and better luck next time.' But nobody came round – not Berger, or the author, or the director, or anybody. They can all run away at a time like that, but the actors have to stay and face it. . . . Oh, my screen test? Oh, I'm not counting on that. They might take Jean. She's got that camera face. But they'll never burn up the Coast wires over me. . . . (*Throwing herself on a bed.*) Oh, how do you know who's an actress, and who isn't! You're an actress if you're acting. Without a job and those lines to say, an actress is just an ordinary person, trying not to look as scared as she feels. What is there about it anyway? Why do we all keep trying? . . . The idiotic part of it is that I didn't feel so terrible after the first minute. I thought, well, Keith's coming round after the show and we'll go to Smitty's and sit there and talk and it won't seem so bad. But he never showed up. . . . I don't expect him to be like other people. I wouldn't want him to be. One of the things that makes him so much fun is that he's different. If he forgets an appointment it's because he's working and doesn't notice. Only I wish he had come tonight. (*She starts undressing.*) I needed him so. (*Suddenly her defences are down.*) Kaye, I'm frightened. For the first time, I'm frightened. It's three years now. The first year it didn't matter so much. I was so young. Nobody was ever as young as I was. I thought, they just don't know. But I'll get a good start and show them. I didn't mind anything in those days. Not having any money, or quite enough food; and a pair of silk stockings always a major investment. I didn't mind because I felt sure that that wonderful part was going to come along. But it hasn't. And suppose it doesn't next year? Suppose it never comes?

Summerfolk
Maxim Gorky

Varvara is 27, married to an older husband, Sergei Basov. At this stage in the play, in the country for the Summer, she is disillusioned, angry and frustrated by the behaviour and attitudes of the bourgeois circle she finds herself in. The scene takes place on the lawn and terrace of their Summer house. It is early evening, 1904, and Varvara is suddenly moved to speak her feelings to the assembled company.

Gorky put his own viewpoint into the character of Varvara, wishing to show that section of the Russian intelligentsia that emerged from the working people, gained social status, but lost contact with its roots, forgetting the needs of the people, the necessity of broadening their lives. When first performed it caused a stir amongst the very people it depicted.

VARVARA (*suddenly, with irritation, after listening to conversation around her.*) The intelligentsia! . . . We're not the intelligentsia . . . we're something quite different. We're just the summerfolk of this country . . . who've just dropped by from somewhere else. We bustle about looking for comfortable little nests for ourselves – and do nothing else but talk a ridiculous amount. . . . (*Her irritation growing, as the others start listening to her.*) . . . And our conversations are full of lies. We hide our spiritual bankruptcy from each other by dressing ourselves up in fine phrases and the tattered remnants of secondhand wisdom . . . we go on about how tragic life is without ever having experienced it . . . we just love whining and groaning and complaining . . . oh, let's have an end to complaining, let's have the courage to keep silent! We keep silent easily enough when life seems satisfying, don't we? We all gobble up our little bits of happiness alone and in secret, but as soon as there's the tiniest little scratch on our hearts, we rush out into the streets with it and show it to everybody and weep and groan about our pain to anyone who'll listen! Just as we poison the air of our towns with the garbage we throw out of our houses, so we poison other people's lives with the trash and nastiness that pours out of our souls. I'm sure that hundreds and thousands of perfectly healthy people must perish through being bludgeoned and deafened by our poisonous complainings . . . Who gave us the right to poison other people with a display of our own personal sores and ulcers? . . . (*She breaks off, realising the effect she has made, and looks round bewildered.*) . . . I seem to have said something . . . something wrong? Was I rude? . . . Why is everyone so strange?

Translated by Jeremy Brooks and Kitty Hunter Blair

The Winter Wife
Claire Tomalin

Based on the life of the New Zealand-born writer, and wife of John Middleton Murry, Katherine Mansfield (1888–1923). In this scene it is Autumn, 1920, in the salon of the Villa Isola Bella, a holiday house in Menton, on the French Riviera. Katherine is 31, abroad with a companion, Ida Baker (Jones) a spinster who adores her and is over-anxious, too kind, very sensible and described by Katherine as 'an irritant in my daily life'. Here she is talking to Dr Bouchage, an intelligent English-speaking doctor. Katherine's life is full of problems, an uneasy marriage at times, fear of blackmail from a past relationship, her tuberculosis and the diagnosis of venereal disease. Bouchage advises her to go north into Switzerland in Spring and allow Miss Baker to care for her saying: 'I believe she knows how to look after you quite well'.

KATHERINE. Miss Baker. (*Laughing.*) You want me to lose a husband and gain a wife. I shall have to think about all this. (*Pause.*) Dr Bouchage, I told you that I am a writer. I have, on your advice, given up the work I was doing for my husband's magazine. That doesn't matter. But now I have to write for *myself*. You understand what I mean? You have seen me over these months at Menton. You know something about me – something of my temperament, something of my history; some of the bad things that have happened to me. I have things I want to write. *If* I do not have long to live, I want to spend the time I have in saying – or in starting to say – what I know about the world. About men and women. About human indifference and cruelty and stupidity. About the way in which people devour one another, and poison one another. About the importance of hate. (*Pause.*) There are

134

so many things I want to describe! What it is to like to be an ordinary, healthy woman – Marie, say, going to the market under the green and gold shade of the plane trees, through streets that smell of lemons and fresh coffee – past cafes where lovers who imagine they are happy are sitting under the pink and white umbrellas – past the fountain where she stops to talk to other ordinary, healthy women with their water pots – feeling on their faces and arms the warm wind off the sea. The treacherous sea. All this, all this: and to know in your own bones nothing but suffering and death.

Pause. BOUCHAGE *is looking at her intently, and listening.*

And you, Doctor Bouchage: you know very well what I mean, I believe. All this time you have been plumbing my depths, finding out my secrets, I have been observing you too, and finding out yours. You may be the doctor, but I am the writer. And just as you can tell me things about myself, I can tell you something about yourself. You know that my life is burning away – more or less quickly – but I know that you are also touched by the same burning frost. I can see it in your eyes and feel it when you touch me with your good, sensitive fingers. You are too quick, too kind, too responsive, too eager. If you are a good doctor, it is because you are almost as sick as I am.

Diana of Dobson's
Cicely Hamilton

Diana was a shop assistant at Dobson's Drapery Emporium, when she was left a small legacy. She decided to use it on travelling and the good life for a while but it is now all spent. The time is 1908 at the Hotel Engadine, Pontresina, and Diana is talking to Captain Bretherton, another guest there who, believing her to be a wealthy widow, has just made a proposal of marriage.

DIANA. Oh, I'm Diana Massingberd right enough. That's my name – my legal and lawful name – and the only thing about me that isn't a snare and delusion. . . . I'm perfectly sane. All I'm trying to do is to make you understand that instead of being a rich widow, I'm a poor spinster – a desperately poor spinster. . . . I've been taking you in, of course. . . . You and all your friends – sailing under false colours. No doubt it was a disgraceful thing to do – but before you get angry with me, I have a right to ask you to hear my story – (*More rapidly and with less self-control as her feelings get the better of her.*) My father was a country doctor – an underpaid country doctor. When he died there was nothing – nothing at all – and I was thrown upon my own resources for a living. I earned it how and when I could – and a little more than a month ago I was a shop assistant in London. . . . My last situation was at Dobson's – a big draper's. I was in the hosiery department. . . . Earning five shillings a week and having a hell of a time. I shan't apologise for the unparliamentary expression – it is justified. I'd had six years of that sort of slavery – been at it since my father died. Then one night I got a solicitor's letter, telling me that a distant cousin of mine was dead, and that I had come in for three hundred pounds. . . . Of course, if I'd been a sensible woman I should have hoarded up my windfall – invested it in something safe and got three per cent for it. But I didn't. I was sick of the starve and the stint and the grind of it all – sick to death of the whole grey life – and so I settled to have a royal time while the money lasted. All the things that I'd wanted – wanted horribly, and couldn't have – just because I was poor – pretty dresses, travel, amusement, politeness, consideration, and yes, I don't mind confessing it – admiration – they should be mine while the cash held out. I knew that I could buy them – every one – and I wasn't wrong – I have bought them. I've had my royal time. I've been petted and admired and made much of – and enjoyed it down to the very ground. . . . And now it's over – and the money's spent and . . . I'm going back. To work. To the old life and the old grind. . . . Well – now you know the whole story – and having heard it you are no doubt feeling very much obliged to me because I refused to allow you to commit yourself a few minutes ago. . . . An adventuress? So I'm an adventuress, am I? Doesn't this rather remind you of the celebrated interchange of compliments between the pot and kettle? . . . For if I'm an adventuress, Captain Bretherton, what are you but an adventurer?

Boid Girls
Rona Munro

The play is set in a troubled area of Belfast where roadblocks, gunfire and shootings are part of everyday life. It deals with the lives of women whose husbands have been either killed or imprisoned for their political activities. Marie is 33, with two young sons, her husband Michael was killed over three years ago. Still lively, and attractive, she spends time dreaming of him, although, as she says, she knows 'he was no saint'. His photograph hangs on the wall. For this speech the lights are centred on Marie as she remembers her wedding day, 16 years ago.

Time: 1990.

MARIE. It was a terrible wet day when I got married. A wet grey day in nineteen seventy-four and I couldn't get to the church for the road blocks. I was standing out on my step there with my mummy screaming at me to come before I got my good white dress dirty from the rain – only I was wetter from crying than the clouds could make me, because Michael Donnelly was the only boy I'd ever wanted for myself and me just seventeen. He was the only boy I'd wanted at all and it was still a miracle to me he wanted me back – but then since I've always had to work hardest at believing miracles and anyway I knew they only fell in the laps of the pure in heart, now it seemed certain to me that a pile of Brits and a road block would lose me Michael altogether – for why would he wait an hour or more at the church, when he'd that smile on him that made you feel wicked and glad about it and that look to him that caught your eye when he was walking down the street. Just with the way he put his feet down, bold and happy together, and those hands that were so warm and gentle you hardly worried where he was putting them and why would a man like that wait two hours in a cold church for a wee girl in a damp wedding dress? (*Pause.*) And my mummy's trying to pull my daddy in 'cause he's shouting at the Brits saying this was the greatest day of his daughter's life and hadn't they just spoiled it altogether? Then this big Saracen's pulled up and they've all jumped out and my mummy's just going to scream when do they not offer us an escort through the road block? So that was my bridal car to the wedding, a big Saracen full of Brits all grinning and offering us fags and pleased as punch with themselves for the favour they were doing us. I hardly dared look at them. I was certain the big hulk next to me was one of them that had lifted Michael just the year before but oh they were nice as anything. There was wanted men at the wedding and everything. Sure I'd grey hairs before I was ever married. And then I was married and Michael brought me here and the rain stopped; it even looked like the sun had come out and I stared and stared, just standing at the top of the path in my wee white dress that was still half soaked. I felt like we'd won through everything, the weather and the road blocks and the Brits and there were never going to be bad times again – because I was never going to be without him again. Well – I was just seventeen after all.

Golden Girls
Louise Page

This play is centred around a group of highly ambitious female athletes. Obsessed with their own sporting careers they have lost all interest in the outside world to become isolated in their own athletic microcosm. Hilary Davenport, a smart assertive businesswoman is the team's sponsor and a representative of 'Golden Girls' shampoo. Determined to promote the team image and consequently the image of the brand, she advises the girls on how best to improve their public relations techniques.

HILARY. I'd like to spend a few minutes with you on the do's and don'ts of being the Golden Girls squad. We don't believe that sponsors should interfere with their er – there's not really a word for it – those we're sponsoring. But if you work for any organisation there are a few ground rules. I've brought with me several crates of Golden Girls shampoo and from now on I'd ask you only to use Golden Girls. I've brought up your tracksuits and running togs. I know yellow doesn't suit everybody – But I think our designers have managed to find a shade that will do justice to all of you. We're keen for you to wear these at all times. I know that some of you have certain affinities to various articles of clothing but I hope you'll be able to re-invest those in the Golden Girls kit. No one wants to lay down rules of behaviour to grown women but I think you must all realise that being a Golden Girl has certain responsibilities. Obviously we want winners but if you don't win, don't forget the glory there is to be obtained by being a good loser. The joy of the race is in the running after all. I think we'd all agree that we wouldn't look up to a heroine who swears like a trooper, even if she has just lost. I needn't stress how important it is for you to stress that you are sponsored by us. That as athletes you are assisted by us for the money that allows you to compete and a little that we put into your trust funds but nothing more. No one wants to hear the dirty rustle of five pound notes. The last thing I want to say is you'll find it difficult in interviews – people will do everything they can to avoid you mentioning the name of the product. But the more accidental slips you make the more you help our sales and consequently what we can invest in you. It can become a little game. We're going to reward you with an extra £100 in your trust funds every time you manage to mention Ortolan or Golden Girls. Most of all I want you to enjoy the benefits that Ortolan's sponsorship can give you and to put everything you can towards first Gateshead and Crystal Palace and then triumphing in Athens. Do that and we'll see where we can go from there.

Map of the Heart
William Nicholson

Dr Mary Hanlon is giving a talk to a hall full of hospital doctors. Dr Albie Steadman is fired with enthusiasm to accompany her to the Sudan to do charitable work and the two become lovers. Albie is captured and taken hostage, leaving his lover and his wife to explore their feelings about him. Mary is an intense woman in her early thirties, neither pretty nor plain. The conviction that illuminates her face as she speaks in this early scene from the play gives her presence real charisma.
  Time: The present.

MARY. This is not an appeal for money. It's an appeal for lives. I'm not here to ask you for charity, or to make you feel guilty. I'm here to ask you one simple question: are you leading the life you want to lead? If your answer is yes, then what I have to say won't be of any interest to you. You might as well leave now. I won't mind. (*She pauses to see if any want to leave.*) No one ever does leave. I used to think that meant everyone was eager to change their lives, but once, after I gave this talk in Hammersmith, a junior registrar came up to me and thanked me warmly, and when I said 'Will you be joining us in the camps?' he said no, he just felt so much better knowing there was somewhere worse than Charing Cross Hospital. I work in a field hospital in a large refugee camp near a town called Juba, in the south of Sudan. The population of the camp divides crudely into three. One third is dying of starvation. Another third is seriously malnourished and dying of infectious diseases: dysentry, cholera, typhoid. The final third is reasonably healthy, and killing each other in a civil war. So you won't be surprised to hear that the question I'm most often asked is, why bother? You read the papers. This year the drought is the worst ever, the disaster the largest ever. Ten million facing starvation; fifteen million. It's true, and at the same time, it's too much. The sheer scale of the tragedy makes people block their ears and shut their eyes. What can I say? That I'm bringing the suffering to an end? I wish I was. That I'm saving lives? A few, perhaps, but for what? For the war? For the famine? The truth is, I haven't got an answer. It's just become my work. It's what I do. But let me ask you the same question about your life. Why do you bother? Are you leading the life you want to lead? When it's over, will you look back and say, that wasn't what I wanted to do at all? . . . That's not how it is for me. For five years now I've known the greatest freedom life has to offer. If I die tomorrow, I'll be able to say, I lived the life I wanted to live. Will you?

Mother Said I Never Should
Charlotte Keatley

The play is about four generations of women living this century in London and Manchester. In 1971, 19-year-old Jackie had an illegitimate baby, Rosie. Her mother, Margaret and father, Ken, bring Rosie up as their own child, but when Margaret dies in 1987 Rosie finds her birth certificate. Here, Rosie has just accused Jackie of wanting her own life more than she wanted a child.

Setting: The garden of Ken and Margaret's suburban semi, in Rayne's Park, London, early morning, just after Margaret's death.

Time: 1987.

JACKIE. How dare you! (*Goes to hit* ROSIE *but cannot.*) You're at the centre of everything I do! (*Slight pause.*) Mummy treated me as though I'd simply fallen over and cut my knee – picked me up and said you'll be all right now, it won't show much. She wanted to make it all better. (*Quiet.*) . . . She was the one who wanted it kept secret . . . I WANTED you, Rosie. (*Angry.*) For the first time in my life I took care of myself – refused joints, did exercises, went to the clinic. (*Pause.*) 'It's a girl.' (*Smiles irresistibly.*) – After you'd gone I tried to lose that memory. (*Pause. Effort.*) Graham . . . your father. (*Silence.*) He couldn't be there the day you were born, he had to be in Liverpool. He was married. (*Emphatic.*) He loved me, he loved you, you must believe that! (*Pause.*) He said he'd leave his wife, but I knew he wouldn't; there were two young children, the youngest was only four . . . we'd agreed, separate lives, I wanted to bring you up. He sent money. (*Pause.*) I took
144

you to Lyme Park one day, I saw them together, across the lake, he was buying them ice creams, his wife was taking a photo. I think they live in Leeds now, I saw his name in the Guardian last year, an article about his photographs . . . (*Pause.*) It was a very cold winter after you were born. There were power cuts. I couldn't keep the room warm; there were no lights in the tower blocks; I knew he had an open fire, it was trendy; so we took a bus to Didsbury, big gardens, pine kitchens, made a change from concrete. I rang the bell. (*Stops.*) A Punjabi man answered, said he was sorry . . . they'd moved. By the time we got back to Mosside it was dark, the lift wasn't working – (*Stops.*) That was the night I phoned Mummy. (*Difficult.*) Asked her. (*Pause.*) I tried! I couldn't do it, Rosie. (*Pause.*) It doesn't matter how much you succeed afterwards, if you've failed once. (*Pause.*) After you'd gone . . . I kept waking in the night to feed you . . . A week . . . in the flat . . . Then I went back to art school. Sandra and Hugh thought I was inhuman. I remember the books that came out that winter – how to succeed as a single working mother – fairytales! (*Pause.*) Sandra and Hugh have a family now. Quite a few of my friends do. (*Pause.*) I could give you everything now. Rosie? . . .

The Man Who Came to Dinner
George S Kaufman and Moss Hart

Sheridan Whiteside, a larger than life personality is confined to a wheelchair in the home of friends, following an accident. He continues to conduct his busy life from there, monopolising the household. Amongst the extrovert personalities from all walks of life who visit him is film-star, Lorraine Sheldon. Sheridan's secretary, Maggie, dislikes her, believing she will destroy her chances of a relationship with writer, Bert Jefferson, so she conspires with actor Beverley Carlton to get rid of her with a hoax telephone call in which he impersonates the rich English Lord Bottomley proposing marriage. Lorraine is described as 'the most chic actress on the London or New York stage . . . she glitters as she walks . . . beautiful . . . glamorous . . . one of the Ten Best-Dressed Women of the World . . . in short, a siren of no mean talents, and knows it.' In this scene, she has just discovered the hoax.

Place: The sitting room of a comfortable house in Ohio, America.

Time: 1939.

LORRAINE. Sherry, I want this explained. . . . Why would Beverley want to do such a thing? This is one of the most dreadful – oh, my God! Those cables! Those cables! (*To phone.*) Give me the hotel – whatever it's called – I want the hotel. . . . I'll pay him off for this if it's the last thing I – why, the skunk! – the louse! The dirty rotten – Mansion House? Connect me with the maid. . . . What? . . . Who the hell do you *think* it is? Miss Sheldon, of course. . . . Oh, God! Those cables. If only Cosette hasn't – Cosette! Cosette! Did you send those cables? . . . Oh, God! Oh, God! . . . Now, listen. Cosette, I want you to send another cable to every one of those people, and tell them somebody
146

has been using my name, and to disregard anything and everything they hear from me – except this, of course. . . . Don't ask questions – do as you're told. . . . Don't argue with me, you French bitch – God damn it, do as you're told . . . and unpack, we're not going! (*She hangs up . . . turning to* WHITESIDE's *wheelchair.*) What do you mean take it easy? Do you realise I'll be the laughing stock of England? Why, I won't dare show my face! I always knew Beverley Carlton was low, but not this low. Why? WHY? It isn't even funny. Why would he do it, that's what I'd like to know. Why would he do it! Why would anyone in the world want to play a silly trick like this? I can't understand it. Do you, Sherry? Do you, Maggie? You both saw him this afternoon. Why would he walk out of here, go right to a phone booth and try to ship me over to England on a fool's errand! There must have been some reason – there must have. It doesn't make sense otherwise. Why should Beverley Carlton, or anybody else for that matter, want me to? (*She looks at* MAGGIE . . . *then at the door through which* BERT JEFFERSON *has gone . . . then back to* MAGGIE.) I – I think I begin to – of course! Of course! That's it. Of course that's it. Yes, and that's a very charming bracelet that Mr Jefferson gave you – isn't it, Maggie dear? Of course. It makes complete sense now. And to think that I nearly – well! Wild horses couldn't get me out of here *now*. (*Crossing to* MAGGIE.) Maggie, and if I were you I'd hang on to that bracelet, dear. It'll be something to remember him by. . . . (JEFFERSON *re-enters.*) Mr Jefferson, I'm not leaving after all. My plans are changed. . . . And I hear you've written a simply marvellous play, Mr Jefferson. I want you to read it to me – tonight. Will you? We'll go back to the Mansion House right after dinner. And you'll read me your play.

Our Day Out
Willy Russell

Mrs Kay and Mr Briggs have taken a class of 14-year-olds on a day trip to Wales. The children are all from the 'Progress Class' of a comprehensive in the backstreets of Liverpool, most of them have no aims in life and their futures are depressingly empty and bleak. But this day has given them a chance to let loose for once and play havoc. Mrs Kay tries to persuade her colleague that not all the benefits of such a day have to be educational.

MRS KAY. Pardon me. What's got to stop? . . . (*Quietly.*) I was just thinking; it's a shame really isn't it? We bring them out to a crumbling pile of bricks and mortar and they think they're in the fields of heaven. Well I'd suggest that if you want the chaos to stop you should simply look at it not as chaos but what it actually is – kids, with a bit of space around them, making a bit of noise. All right, so the head asked you to come along – but can't you just relax? There's no point in pretending that a day out to Wales is going to be of some great educational benefit to them. It's too late for them. Most of these kids were rejects the day they came into the world. We're not going to solve anything today Mr Briggs. Can't we just give them a good day out? Mm? At least we could try and do that. (*Beginning to let her temper go.*) Well what's your alternative? Eh? Pretending? Pretending that they've got some sort of future ahead of them? Even if you cared for these kids you couldn't help to make a future for them. You won't educate them because nobody wants them educating. . . . No you listen Mr Briggs, you listen and perhaps you'll stop fooling yourself. Teach them? Teach
148

them what? You'll never teach them because nobody knows what to do with them. Ten years ago you could teach them to stand in line, you could teach them to obey, to expect little more than a lousy factory job. But now they haven't even got that to aim for. Mr Briggs, you won't teach them because you're in a job that's designed and funded to fail! There's nothing for them to do, any of them; most of them were born for factory fodder, but the factories have closed down. I'm not going to let you prevent the kids from having some fun. If you want to abandon this visit you'd better start walking because we're not going home. We're going down to the beach! (*She walks away.*) Colin, round everybody up. Come on everybody, we're going to the beach. You can't come all the way to the seaside and not pay a visit to the beach.

The Passing-Out Parade
Anne Valery

A play about a group of ATS girls in the Second World War from their recruitment to their passing-out parade. In this scene Sergeant Joyce Pickering is instructing them in the salute. . . . Pickering is described 'In her 40's. Born in Worcestershire, she joined the ATS on the first day of the war as her father joined the army in 1914. Cares passionately for classical music; collects boxes but has nothing to put in them. Immaculately turned out and has dealt with such recruits many times before; always using the same mock gaiety, the same speech, peppering it with French phrases at times.'

Scene: Outside the Barrack Room.

Time: Early 1944.

The author suggests that the speech could be performed in your choice of dialect.

PICKERING (*after saluting smartly to the departing CO and waiting until she is out of earshot turns to opposite direction and shouts to the recruits she is training*). . . . Right, me anguished amateurs. You've just hobserved a salute, so let me start as I mean to go on – and on – and on. Forward, ten paces – march! (*The GIRLS enter.*) Halt. And face front. And (*She demonstrates.*) – stand – at – ease! I said 'stand!' Not disintegrate. Now you're to watch my every move as if your miserable lives depended on it, which they very well might! A recruit will – at all times, mark me – salute an hofficer. AT ALL TIMES do you hear me? Doesn't matter if you're starkers or on the bog. . . . (*One of the GIRLS giggles.*) Go on like that and you'll be laughing the other side of nowhere. So – when you see an hofficer – female or male – you salute. IS THAT CLEAR? . . . (*Their answer is not loud enough or*
150

correct. She cups her hand to her ear.) YES, SERGEANT,
and let it ring in me ear like the last trump. (*They shout
this time. She smiles.*) And now to the salute. . . . A salute
is in three parts. . . . Each part to the count of three. Each
part to the count of three. One, two, three – up. (*Arm up.*)
One, two, three – hold. (*Salutes.*) Note the palm facing
front, fingers stiff as stanchions. One, two, three – down.
(*Hand to side.*) The more hobservant amongst you will have
regard to the fact that the way my harm goes up is like a
ruddy rainbow. Down it is stuck to my body as if drawn
there by a magnet. (*Banging her thumb against her skirt.*)
Thumbs down seams! Right! I will now demonstrate once
again. And only the once. The longest way up, two three.
Hold, two, three. The shortest way down, two, three. So
– you will now follow my every miniscule move, shouting
the numbers as if to Moscow, first marking yourselves
by stretching arms out to both sides so you don't knock
yourselves out – before I do. AND I MIGHT. Right then
– tenshun! And – mark. . . . (*Watching them.*) Crab! You
are not the Ziegfield Follies about to high kick to kingdom
come, so . . . uncoil yourself, girl! (*She walks behind line
of* GIRLS *observes a large gap in the line, and fuming, steps
through it.*) Forming a company of our own are we? Close
up! (*To whole line.*) And . . . arms down! And prepare to
salute, shouting the numbers . . . one, two, three, as you
do so. . . . (*Counting with them.*) One, two, three . . . up.
One, two, three . . . hold. One, two, three . . . down . . .
(*The* GIRLS *are terrible. Silence.*) Yes, well, and so perhaps
we'll have better luck calling our army numbers – starting
with Crab. (*Listens while all seven repeat their number.*) What
a little optimist I am! For your information we are not
spotting puff-puff engine numbers, jolly though that might
be. Oh dear me no. We are attempting to identify ourselves
in a clear crisp manner. Do I make myself clear so that you
will make yourselves crystal? . . . So, aprés moi, le deluge!

Numbers repeat! (*This time they are a little better.*) And –
salute. . . . Up, two, three. Hold, two, three. Down, two,
three. . . . (*They are still terrible.*) WE ARE NOT, repeat
NOT, training to be the Corps de Ballet de Pontefract!
Glad you see it my way. So – ruddy salute. (*Very fast.*)
Up, one two, three. Hold, one, two, three. Down, one,
two, three. . . . (*Looking at watch.*) Heigh ho, how time
flies when one's having fun. So. Company – by the left,
right turn. Company, chests out, sit-a-pons in. Forward –
march. Left, right, left, right, left, right. (*Watches* GIRLS
go, noting JENKINS *is on wrong foot.*) Jenkins! LEFT, right.
LEFT, right. LEFT, right. (*She marches out behind them.*)

Womberang
Sue Townsend

The scene is set in a hospital outpatients' waiting room where the afternoon gynaecological clinic is in progress. About six people are waiting to be seen. Rita, an outspoken woman has just escorted another patient to the lavatory, leaving her friend Dolly on the front bench, talking to a woman beside her. Dolly is a housewife and mother. At one point Rita talks about Dolly's life and her husband: 'Dolly thinks he will come back, don't you Dolly? She thinks he'll leave his posh flat and his page-three bird to come back to his council house and three screaming kids. . . .'

Time: The present.

DOLLY (*proudly*). I'm her best friend. . . . Yes, she's a case isn't she? You wouldn't have known her last year. Her husband walked all over her, got so bad she wouldn't go out of the house, kids did all the shopping, she sat by the fire watching telly all day then cleaned the house over and over when the kids were in bed. Not normal is it? Anyway, her doctor sent her to the Towers, got an order from the court, she wouldn't go voluntary, wouldn't leave the kids. But oh, you should have seen her at the end, like a wild woman she was. *I* had to go in and feed the kids, do the washing and all that. She sat in a chair filthy, watching the telly, didn't speak a word to nobody, then one night one of the kids burnt themselves on the stove making some toast. Reet never moved, didn't turn her head. They took the kids away that night, in care they call it. I told them I'd have them, but they said we was already overcrowded anyway. Reet goes in the Towers like a zombie and comes out like you've seen her today. . . . Yes, she did have the

153

electric shock, but it wasn't that, it was the therapy group. Therapy, that's where they all sit around and tell everyone in the group what they really think, really think! Like say if someone's got dirty teeth, they tell them . . .

The SITTERS *all become teeth-conscious.*

. . . I think you should clean your teeth. Awful isn't it? Or if they've got a bogy in their nose . . . you tell them, you tell them all about when you were a kid. If your husband drives you mad when he's eating. Things you wouldn't normally tell nobody. Reet was quiet at first, didn't talk much, then somebody said her roots needed doing, she's not a natural blonde – but don't say anything. Well Reet went wild, called him everything from a pig to a cow. After that she's been the same as you saw her today, speaks her mind, does things instead of sitting quiet. But she's a good friend to me. F'rinstance, my baker's been fiddling me for years. You know what they do, charge you for cakes you haven't had, leave bread you haven't ordered, it soon mounts up. Reet made me tell him. She stood behind the door. I said, 'I shan't want no more bread.' He said, 'When, this week?' 'No, never,' I says and Reet shot from behind the door and says, 'And she won't be paying this week's bill neither, take it out of what you've fiddled from her over the years.' Well he never said a word, just got into his van and drove off. Oh, it was so lovely not having him call every day, but I did feel a bit sorry for him. (*As* RITA *returns.*) . . . I was telling this lady about you, Rita . . . since your therapy.

Alas, Poor Fred

James Saunders

Mr and Mrs Pringle seem, on the surface, an ordinary, middle-aged couple, living in an ordinary suburb. When the play opens a domestic scene shows him asleep in his easy chair, while she knits in hers. But underneath the conventional clichéd conversation, the seemingly innocent marital bickering, lurks past murder and passion. Left alone for a few minutes while her husband leaves to fetch a photograph with which he hopes to settle an argument, Mrs Pringle releases another side to her character.

Written in 1958, in the theatre of the absurd style.

MRS. Why must it always come to this? . . . Every night is the same. Sometimes I get a feeling of impending doom even before the sun goes down. But the doom never arrives. How is that, I wonder? (*She knits, then stops.*) One thing I hope for. That is, that one evening Ernest will go out of the room for some reason, as he does occasionally during the evening, and that while I am sitting here alone in the quiet room that chair . . . will move. Just a little. I don't want it to move much. Just a foot, or six inches, without any noise or fuss. What a thing that would be . . . Ernest would come back and I should say, Ernest, something happened while you were away. And he'd say nonsense, nothing happened. And I'd say yes, Ernest, *this* time something did happen while you were away. And he'd say, what could happen while I was away? And I'd say, I'll give you three guesses, Ernest, what happened, and if you guess right you can wish for anything you want and I'll make it come true, and he'd say, did the clock stop? No, that's one. Did the picture slip out of square? No, Ernest darling, the picture didn't slip

155

out of square, and that's two. Now here's your last one and you must guess carefully because if you guess wrong I shall have to tell you and you won't believe me and you won't get your wish either, and he'd say, well now, I guess that that chair . . . moved. Yes, darling, I'd say, yes, darling, Ernest darling, that's just exactly what happened. That's just exactly what happened, darling Ernest darling, you have your wish. Who cares about old chairs. Take me in your arms, darling Ernest darling, and do with me what thou wilt. . . . But it never does, needless to say.

She knits.

Reserved
David Campton

This two-hander takes place in a restaurant and involves a heated conversation between two middle-aged women, the Shopper and the Waitress. The Shopper has insisted on remaining at a reserved table, complete with her full heavy shopping bags. She is a shapeless, shabby person and at the start of this speech is taking a variety of purchases from her bag . . . family-size cornflakes, washing powder, biscuits, toilet rolls etc.

Time: The present.

SHOPPER. Family-size for the family house. Giant-size for the giants' house. Fun-size for the funny house. . . .

Finally she fishes out a battered cigarette packet . . . takes out a cigarette and lights it. After a few puffs she realises that there are other people at other tables. She talks partly to them and partly to herself, not expecting u reply.

I'm not upsetting you with this, am I? . . . I don't often smoke at table . . . I don't often smoke at all. That's why the packet was at the bottom of the bag. . . . You're sure I'm not annoying anybody? You've only got to say and I'll put it out. . . . After all, I've had my couple of puffs. . . . I don't really enjoy it after that first couple of puffs. . . . Come to think, I don't really like smoking at all. It's more like a hankering. And once you've had it, you don't really want it, if you know what I mean. . . . It's the same with chocolate eclairs. I don't know why I asked for a chocolate eclair. Only you can't sit in a place like this without asking for something, and a chocolate eclair was all I could think of. . . . I don't know why. I don't often think of chocolate

157

eclairs. I don't really *like* chocolate eclairs. As a child I was never allowed to have a chocolate eclair. In some respects I had a deprived childhood. 'You don't want one of them,' my mother would say. 'You want a Nelson square.' So I'd have a Nelson square. . . . Very filling, Nelson squares. . . . I haven't had one for years. Only you can't come into a place like this and ask for a Nelson square. This isn't a Nelson square sort of place. Not my sort of place, really. This is more of an eclair sort of place. I suppose my Mam was right after all. I'm not an eclair sort of person. I'm more of a Nelson square sort of person. When you've been brought up on Nelson squares, you just don't come into this sort of place. . . . I didn't mean to go on. I don't suppose you know what I'm on about anyway. I bet you wouldn't even know what a Nelson square looks like. . . . Well, you mince last week's cake, mix with fruit and sandwich between two slabs of pastry. That's a Nelson square. Very filling. . . . Mind you, I don't know what Nelson had to do with them. Unless he invented them. Though I can't make out why he should – him being a sailor. It might have been a different person of the same name and in the cake business. . . . Yes, I suppose that's the sort of person I am. Leftovers and pastry. (*She stubs out her cigarette.*) I'm not going to enjoy a chocolate eclair after that. After that I'm not even going to *taste* a chocolate eclair.

158

Ask For The Moon
Shirley Gee

In this play the women working in a lacemaker's cottage in 1840
*are contrasted with those in a modern East End sweatshop. Lil,
a brave, gutsy, funny-sad, elderly woman has worked in the
sweatshop for* 58 *years, originally under the present manager's
father. Now her work is failing seriously; she slyly exchanges
poor garments for another woman's superior work. She has been
caught stealing buttons and in a moment of anger and despair has
removed all her clothing except her underwear, finishing with her
blouse of which she says scornfully: 'Cheap fabric. Seconds. Isn't
even on the grain.'*

LIL. Remnant. Left in a corner. Thrown out in the end.
Like me. I got a prize at my school for smocking. Did I tell
you, Annie? . . . Wish I was young now. Wish I was still at
school. Fifty-eight years I been here. . . . (*To* EUGENE, *the
boss.*) See me. Acknowledge me. I'm not who I was. Course
I'm not. But at my own speed I still got the skill. . . . But
nobody wants it, do they? Not any more. You could have
saved me. You could have said, no one can touch your
smocking, Lil, your buttonholes is perfect. But now we
got machines can do it just as good – well, maybe not
as good, but it looks all right, we'll get away with it. So
seeing as you're so special at it, what we'll do, we'll teach
you something else you can be good at, something these
things can't do. We'll educate you. Train you. But no one
ever said that, did they? Not your father, and not you. . . .
That's not sewing is it? That's feeding a machine. No time to
think. No time to make a proper job of it. Just sit there with
your heart banging in your ears and them things screeching.

Stop knowing who you are and what you are and who you used to be. Who was I, Eugene? Was I really someone? . . . Now I'm sub-ordinary. Now I'm getting 37p. . . . What am I supposed to do? Live on a box of cottons and my memories? What have I done wrong? Except get a bit older. Will one of you please tell me? What have I done wrong? . . . I work my guts out for you – and all I am's a hiccup on your production line. You bastard, Eugene, you rotten, stinking bastard. You've left me on the sand. You've took my skill away and left me on the sand and I got nothing. A stupid old carcass to lug about all day. And nothing. A smile, a slap on the rump, a cup of tea. Nothing. . . . It's you that doesn't understand. Not one of you. Look. These hands is just a cover. My real hands is inside them. And they're stitching away, quick, quick, quick. Fifty-eight years I've sat there. All my working years. I've stitched my life away for you. You've broken my whole life. . . . (*As* ANWHELA *comes to her.*) Leave me alone. Leave me alone. For God's sake. All of you. . . . Please. You've got to. Please.

Play Sources

Adam Bede by George Eliot. Out of copyright. (Penguin, also available in various classical novel series. Dramatic adaptation by Geoffrey Beevers, Samuel French.)

The Adoption Papers by Jackie Kay, poetry (Bloodaxe)

Alas, Poor Fred by James Saunders (one-act play) (Samuel French)

Albert's Bridge by Tom Stoppard (one-act play) (Faber and Faber, UK; Grove Press Inc. USA)

All Things Nice by Sharman Macdonald (Faber and Faber)

The Arcata Promise by David Mercer in *Huggy Bear & Other Plays* (out of print) due to be published in 1994 in *Mercer Plays: Two* (Methuen Drama)

Arden of Faversham, Anon. Out of copyright. (New Mermaid series, A & C Black)

Ask for the Moon by Shirley Gee (Faber and Faber)

The Black Prince by Iris Murdoch, novel (Samuel French)

Bleak House by Charles Dickens. Out of copyright. (Penguin, also various classical novel series)

Bold Girls by Rona Munro (Nick Hern Books; acting edition by Samuel French)

A Boston Story by Ronald Gow (Warner Chappel)

Brand by Henrik Ibsen, trans. Michael Meyer, in *Ibsen Plays: Five* (Methuen Drama)

Breaking the Code by Hugh Whitemore (Amber Lane Press; acting edition by Samuel French)

Brother in the Land by Robert Swindells, novel (Oxford University Press and Puffin Books)

The Burston Drum by Ellen Dryden and Don Taylor (Samuel French)

The Cagebirds by David Campton (Samuel French)

Candida by Bernard Shaw in *Plays Pleasant* (Penguin)

Carving a Statue by Graham Greene (Samuel French)

Chains by Elizabeth Baker in *New Woman Plays* eds. Viv Gardner and Linda Fitzsimmons (Methuen Drama)

Clay by Peter Whelan (Samuel French)

Daisy Pulls It Off by Denise Deegan (Samuel French)

Diana of Dobson's by Cicely Hamilton in *New Woman Plays* eds. Viv Gardner and Linda Fitzsimmons (Methuen Drama)

Dreams of Anne Frank by Bernard Kops (Samuel French)

Five Finger Exercise by Peter Shaffer (Samuel French)

The Gift of a Lamb by Charles Causley (Robson Books)

Golden Girls by Louise Page in *Page Plays: One* (Methuen Drama)

The Gut Girls by Sarah Daniels (Methuen Drama)

Hamp by John Wilson (Samuel French)

Hindle Wakes by Stanley Houghton. Out of copyright. (Hereford Play series, Heinemann Educational Books)

Hush by April De Angelis in *Frontline Intelligence 1: New Plays for the Nineties* ed. Pamela Edwardes (Methuen Drama)

Invisible Friends by Alan Ayckbourn (Faber and Faber)

It's Ralph by Hugh Whitemore (Amber Lane Press)

Keeping Tom Nice by Lucy Gannon (Warner Chappell)

Kes by Barry Hines, a novel (Penguin)

Love for Love by William Congreve. Out of copyright. (New Mermaid series, A & C Black)

Man in Motion by Jan Mark, a novel (Puffin)

The Man Who Came to Dinner by George S Kaufman and Moss Hart (Warner Chappell)

Map of the Heart by William Nicholson (Samuel French)

The Moon's The Madonna by Richard Cameron in *Can't*

Stand Up For Falling Down and The Moon's The Madonna
(Methuen Drama)

My Children, My Africa Athol Fugard (Faber and Faber)

My Mother Said I Never Should by Charlotte Keatley
(Methuen Drama)

National Velvet by Enid Bagnold, a novel (Heinemann, UK
and William Morrow, USA)

Not About Heroes by Stephen Macdonald (Faber and Faber)

The Old Bachelor by William Congreve. Out of copyright.
(A & C Black)

Once a Catholic by Mary O'Malley (Samuel French)

Operation Elvis by C P Taylor in *Live Theatre: Four Plays
for Young People* (Methuen, London – out of print but on
hire from Samuel French)

Orphans by Lyle Kessler (Samuel French)

Our Day Out by Willy Russell (Methuen Drama)

The Passing Out Parade by Anne Valery (Samuel French)

Playing Sinatra by Bernard Kops (Samuel French)

Plenty by David Hare (Faber and Faber)

P'tang, Yang, Kipperbang by Jack Rosenthal (Longman)

Random Thoughts in a May Garden (from *Bye Bye Blues and
Other Plays*) by James Saunders (Amber Lanc Press)

Reserved by David Campton (see Useful Addresses
section)

Rope by Patrick Hamilton (Samuel French)

The Roses of Eyam by Don Taylor (Samuel French)

The Rover by Aphra Behn. Out of copyright. In *Behn: Five
Plays* and in Methuen student edition with notes (MSE)
(Methuen Drama)

Same Old Moon by Geraldine Aron (Samuel French)

Shakers by John Godber and Jane Thornton
(Warner Chappell)

Son of Man by Dennis Potter (Samuel French)

Stage Door by George S Kaufmann and Edna Ferber
(Warner Chappell)

Summerfolk by Maxim Gorky in *Gorky: Five Plays*
(Methuen Drama)

The Three Sisters by Anton Chekhov, trans. Michael Frayn,
also in *Chekhov Plays* (Methuen Drama)

Tokens of Affection by Maureen Lawrence in *Plays by
Women: Nine* ed. Annie Castledine (Methuen Drama)

The Two Noble Kinsmen by John Fletcher and William
Shakespeare. Out of copyright. (Penguin, also various
editions of Shakespeare's plays)

Up'n'Under by John Godber (Amber Lane Press)

Vanity Fair by William Makepeace Thackeray. Out of
copyright. (Penguin, also various classical novel series)

Visiting Hour by Richard Harris (Samuel French)

The Vortex by Noël Coward in *Coward Plays: One*
(Methuen Drama)

When We Are Married by J B Priestley (Samuel French)

Whistle Down the Wind by Mary Hayley Bell (New Portway
series, Chivers Press, Bath)

The Winter Wife by Claire Tomalin (Nick Hern Books)

A Woman Killed with Kindness by Thomas Heywood. Out
of copyright. (New Mermaid series, A & C Black)

Womberang by Sue Townsend in *Bazaar and Rummage,
Groping for Words, Womberang* (Methuen Drama)

Acknowledgements

The editor and publishers gratefully acknowledge permission to reproduce copyright material in this book:

April De Angelis: from *Hush* copyright © 1992, 1993 by April de Angelis. Reprinted by permission of Roger Hancock Ltd. Geraldine Aron: from *Same Old Moon* copyright © 1991 by Geraldine Aron. Reprinted by permission of Alan Brodie Representation on behalf of the author. Alan Ayckbourn: from *Invisible Friends* copyright © 1991 by Alan Ayckbourn. Reprinted by permission of Faber and Faber. Enid Bagnold: from *National Velvet* copyright © 1935 by Enid Bagnold. Reprinted by permission of William Heinemann Ltd, UK and William Morrow, USA. Elizabeth Baker: from *Chains* copyright © 1911 by Elizabeth Baker. Reprinted by permission of Methuen Drama. Mary Hayley Bell: from *Whistle Down The Wind* copyright © 1958 by Mary Hayley Bell. Reprinted by permission of the author. Richard Cameron: *The Moon's The Madonna* copyright © 1991 by Richard Cameron. Reprinted by permission of Methuen Drama. David Campton: from *The Cagebirds* copyright © 1976 by David Campton. Reprinted by permission of the author and Samuel French. From *Reserved* copyright © 1983 by David Campton. Reprinted by permission of the author. (See Useful Addresses.) Charles Causley: from *The Gift of a Lamb* copyright © 1978 by Charles Causley. Reprinted by permission of David Higham Associates Ltd. Anton Chekhov: from *The Three Sisters* translation copyright © 1983 by Michael Frayn. Reprinted by permission of Methuen Drama. Noël Coward: from *The Vortex* copyright © 1925 by Noël Coward. Reprinted by permission of Methuen London. Sarah Daniels: from *The Gut Girls* copyright

Useful Addresses

The extracts included in this book may be performed in class and for festivals and examination without further permission or payment. However, should you wish to perform any scene in a public performance such as a festival prizewinners' concert or an entertainment involving the selling of tickets, further permission must be obtained from the correct source. You will find full details inside the published text and it is essential to adhere to the rules.

As a general rule, the publisher Samuel French Limited controls the amateur performing rights for the plays it publishes as well as the amateur rights for many plays professionally controlled by others.

The following addresses will be of use to teachers and students:

Samuel French, 52 Fitzroy Street, London W1P 6JR
(the same address for the theatre bookshop and the publishing house)

As well as a fully-stocked, comprehensive showroom, they publish a *Guide to Selecting Plays*. Certain plays are available on hire.

Organisations which loan sets of plays:

The Drama Association of Wales, 1st Floor, Chapter Arts
    Centre, Market Road, Canton, Cardiff.
Scottish Community Drama Association, 5 York Place,
    Edinburgh EH1 3EB.

Yorkshire Libraries Joint Music and Drama Service, City of Wakefield Metropolitan District Council, Library Headquarters, Balne Lane, Wakefield, West Yorkshire WF2.

Reference Library:

The National Museum of the Performing Arts (The Theatre Museum) in London, houses a reference libary. This opens at the following times: Tues–Fri: 10.30am to 1pm and 2pm to 4.30pm. It is best to make an appointment, preferably ten days before your intended visit. Plays may be read within the library but not borrowed. Address: 1e Tavistock Street, London WC2 7PA.

Dramatists' Agencies:

Alan Brodie Representation (incorporating Michael Imison Playwrights), 6th Floor, Fairgate House, 78 New Oxford Street, London WC1A 1HB

Casarotto Ramsay & Associates Limited, Waverley House, 7–12 Noel Street, London W1F 8GQ

Judy Daish Associates Limited, 2 St Charles Place, London 210 6EG

Dramatists Play Service, Inc, 440 Park Avenue South, New York NY 10016, USA

Play Publishers:

Amber Lane Press Limited, Church Street, Charlbury, Oxford OX7 3PR

David Campton, 35 Liberty Road, Leicester LE3 8JF

Faber and Faber Limited, 3 Queen Square, London WC1N 3AU

Heinemann Educational Books Limited, Halley Court, Jordan Hill, Oxford OX2 8EJ

Nick Hern Books Limited, The Glasshouse, 49a Goldhawk Road, London W12 8QP

Longman, Pearson Education, Edinburgh Gate, Harlow, Essex CM20 2JE

Methuen Drama. A&C Black Publishers Limited, 38 Soho Square, London W1D 3HB

Penguin Books Limited (also Viking and Puffin), 27 Wrights Lane, London W8 5TZ

Warner Chappell Plays, Josef Weinberger Plays Ltd, 12-14 Mortimer Street, London W1N 7RD